REPRESENTATION AND FORM

REPRESENTATION AND FORM

A STUDY OF ÆSTHETIC VALUES IN REPRESENTATIONAL ART

BY WALTER ABELL

PROFESSOR OF ART, ACADIA UNIVERSITY

Introduction by ARTHUR POPE

PROFESSOR OF ART, HARVARD UNIVERSITY

GREENWOOD PRESS, PUBLISHERS
WESTPORT, CONNECTICUT

Originally published in 1936
by Charles Scribner's Sons, New York

Reprinted with the permission
of Marcelle A. Abell

First Greenwood Reprinting 1971

Library of Congress Catalogue Card Number 79-138573

SBN 8371-5772-2

Printed in the United States of America

TO MY PARENTS

EDWARD WALTER

AND

BERTHA HALSEY ABELL

IN AFFECTIONATE GRATITUDE

INTRODUCTION

In the midst of the confusion of thought which prevails at the present moment as to the function of art, Mr. Abell's discussion of the relation of form and representation is particularly timely; but it is, I believe, also of permanent value as a definite step toward a clearer understanding of the nature of æsthetic values in painting. By its exposition of the different factors the total organization of which makes up the final value of a painting, it should bring to the reader increased understanding and hence fuller enjoyment.

It has long seemed to me that many of the present generation, brought up to judge a picture almost exclusively by its effectiveness on the exhibition wall, have lost much of the pleasure and profit to be obtained from an interest in the art of painting. Moreover, by adopting "effectiveness" as a standard of criticism one arrives at strangely distorted conclusions, whether it be the art of the past or of the present day that is in question.

It may be recognized, to be sure, that the emphasis on effectiveness has in recent years accompanied an increased sensitiveness to essential visual qualities. Nevertheless, pictorial design in any complete sense involves not only organization of pattern in the abstract relation of tones on the surface and organization in the three-dimensional space represented, but also organization in the realm of ideas and in the relation of these factors to each other and to the medium and handling employed. Mr. Abell explains this in a very direct fashion and shows how the richness of intrinsic æsthetic significance is increased by the addition of form (or organization) at successive levels or "strata" of apprehension. Especially original and illuminating is his explanation of the possibility of organization in the relation of the different levels of expression—what he calls "representational form." The diagrams used to symbolize this relation are ingenious and helpful. Although one might quarrel with the classification of specific works, as illustrations of possible distinctions to be made, I think they will be found acceptable.

It should be remembered, of course, that a painting is not necessarily worthless just because the richness of possibilities of organization in all factors is not fully exploited. In many of the paintings produced at the present time effectiveness of abstract pattern may be all that is sought for. Although there may be little in them to reward prolonged examination, if the pattern is satisfactory they may be worth having in their own limited fashion. But recognition of their value should not blind us to the relative value of paintings in which decorative effectiveness is subordinated to organization of content. Emphasis on one or another factor may vary perfectly legitimately according to the purpose of the painter.

It might be said, indeed, that there are two types of painting. In one the work is designed for a particular place and must primarily satisfy its function as part of a whole architectural scheme. In another type it is designed to represent certain objects or certain scenes, supposedly of interest to the painter and the predicated observer, in which the representation and expression are the primary functions. Such a painting serves something of the same purpose as a book. It describes certain real or imaginary scenes and may express ideas of various kinds—lyric, dramatic, and so on. It is, like a book, an entirely independent affair—a thing to be read. If it is effective when hung on a wall as part of a decorative scheme, it is so largely by accident, as a book may, by its binding, fit into the general design of a room.

Thus the Sung painters of China had no intention of making their scroll paintings of landscapes decorative in the ordinary sense. They are not "effective" in the manner of modern paintings when spread out on a wall, as they sometimes are for display in our modern museums. They were intended to be read a little at a time, from beginning to end, like their writings in scroll form. The composition is spatial, and one must, as it were, walk about in them to get the full flavor of their content.

The same thing is true of much other Sung painting. It is true also to some extent of the landscape paintings of the English Water Color School of the late eighteenth and the early nineteenth century. These excite very little interest on the part of the typical "modernist" critic, because they are usually not at all striking when exhibited in a picture gallery. Made primarily for reproduction by engraving in books or portfolios, even the originals must be read at close range while held in the hand and studied in leisurely fashion. This does not mean that they may not be organized in two-dimensional pattern as well as in space and ideas; but this is not the only or even the primary consideration. To judge of such pictures by their effectiveness or ineffectiveness in an exhibition is beside the point.

Mr. Abell's book makes a further appeal to me in that it harmonizes with the quantitative theory of æsthetic values expounded so ably in

INTRODUCTION

Professor Birkhoff's *Æsthetic Measure*[1] and suggested briefly in an article of my own in "Art Studies."[2] I believe that we are on the way toward a more comprehensive understanding of æsthetic theory and that in this connection the present book is a valuable contribution.

Arthur Pope

[1] G. D. Birkhoff, *Æsthetic Measure,* Harvard University Press, 1933.
[2] Harvard University Press, Volume 3 (1925), pp. 133-139.

CONTENTS

INTRODUCTION by Arthur Pope   vii

   I. CURRENT VIEWS ON FORM
       AND SUBJECT–MATTER   1

  II. ÆSTHETIC PREMISES   19

 III. ABSTRACT PLASTIC FORM   26

 IV. PLASTIC GAINS THROUGH REPRESENTATION   56

  V. ÆSTHETIC EFFECTS
       IN ULTRA–PLASTIC REPRESENTATION   62

 VI. ASSOCIATIVE FORM   75

VII. ARE ASSOCIATIVE EFFECTS LEGITIMATE?   93

VIII. REPRESENTATIONAL FORM   121

 IX. REPRESENTATIONAL FORM:
       ASPECTS AND VARIATIONS   135

  X. CONCLUSIONS   162

INDEX   169

ILLUSTRATIONS

FACING PAGE

1. Seventeenth-Century German Textile   38

2. Samarkand Rug (detail).   *Private Collection*   38

3. Picasso. Abstraction   48

4. Picasso. Woman with Mandolin   48

5. Picasso. The Poet   48

6. Brancusi. Bird.   *Museum of Modern Art, New York*   48

7. Twelfth-Century Moorish Textile.   *St. Sernin, Toulouse*   58

8. Cézanne. Mt. Ste. Victoire.   *Barnes Foundation, Merion, Pa.*   58

9. Rembrandt. Portrait of an Old Woman.   *Hermitage, Leningrad*   76

10. Rembrandt. The Painter's Mother.   *Private Collection*   76

11. Titian. Madonna of the Cherries.   *Imperial Gallery, Vienna*   80

12. El Greco. Agony in the Garden.   *Arthur Sachs Collection, Paris*   86

13. Perugino. Agony in the Garden.   *Uffizi, Florence*   86

14. Millais. Lorenzo and Isabella.   *Walker Art Gallery, Liverpool*   108

15. Diagrams Symbolizing Variations of Representational Form   *pages 146, 147*

16. Delacroix. Death of Assurbanipal.   *Louvre, Paris*   *facing page* 160

PREFACE

Without generous help from many sources the present volume could scarcely have been written, and if written, would certainly not have been published at the present time or in its present form. The completion of the work is doubly gratifying because of the opportunity which it brings to thank those who have furthered its progress.

What my discussion owes to earlier students of the subject will be evident from quotations and comments introduced in the text. Of the writers there mentioned, four in particular have influenced my point of view: George Santayana, Charles Mauron, Roger Fry, and Albert C. Barnes. To all of them I owe a debt of gratitude: to Professor Santayana and to Doctor Barnes not only for material relevant to the present problem, but for the foundations of my critical thinking. If my work has involved any unpleasant feature, it has been the necessity of differing, in regard to certain conclusions, from these critics to whom I am most indebted and for whose work I have the greatest respect. I can only hope that such differences are the progressive developments of an evolving tradition and that, to a larger view, they merge in the unity of cumulative change which is essential to life.

My preliminary study of æsthetic values in representational art dates from the spring of 1932. Two years later, with the book itself nearing completion, I enjoyed the privilege of summarizing my results in a paper read at the Twenty-third Annual Meeting of the College Art Association, held in New York, March, 1934. Professor Dewey was then just publishing his *Art As Experience,* a volume which includes a considerable discussion of the subject dealt with in my pages. It may be imagined that I turned with the keenest interest to a work by so eminent an authority on a subject so closely related to my own. I was gratified to find that Professor Dewey's conclusions, though reached by a different method and stated in more general and philosophical terms, were in principle akin to mine. Similar conclusions, I suspect, are being reached by many of those who have wrestled during recent years with the problem of form and subject-matter. Perhaps it may not be too much to hope that some such conclusions represent the crystalizing thought of our period upon a problem which has widely and deeply exercised it.

Writing books, in these times of economic stress, is easier than finding publishers for them. The present volume would now be a manuscript abandoned in my file were it not for help received from both personal and corporate sources. The personal assistance has come primarily from Professor Arthur Pope of Harvard. Professor Pope kindly undertook to read the manuscript during the year in which he served as art adviser to the Carnegie Corporation of New York. It is thus jointly to Professor Pope and the Carnegie Corporation that I am indebted for the opportunity of having the book published at the present time. Professor Pope has further done me the great service of making numerous suggestions for the improvement of the text, and of providing the volume with his generous introduction.

The matter of illustrations in its turn has involved complications not to be overcome without assistance from many sources. Having discussed certain works of art in my text, I supposed that nothing would be simpler than to secure photographs of them suitable for reproduction. As it proved, few undertakings could have been more difficult. I have been helped over these difficulties by willing co-operation on the part of the Photograph Division of the Metropolitan Museum and the Frick Art Reference Library. My thanks are due particularly to Miss Alice Felton at the first named of these institutions, and to Miss Ethelwyn Manning, Librarian of the second. Doctor Rudolf M. Riefstahl of New York University, and Miss Helen Gardner of the Chicago Art Institute, have also given advice concerning possible sources of photographic material.

Doctor Albert C. Barnes has kindly allowed me to reproduce the Cézanne "Mt. Ste. Victoire" from his collection, and Mr. Arthur Sachs has extended me a similar privilege with respect to his El Greco "Agony in the Garden." To the Museum of Modern Art, New York, I owe thanks for a photograph of the Brancusi "Bird" in its collection.

In a few cases, the most diligent search has failed to locate original photographs of the desired works, and I have been obliged to reproduce my illustrations from the plates in other books. In this connection I am grateful to the Propyläen-Verlag for permission to reproduce two Picassos from Einstein's *Die Kunst des 20. Jahrhunderts.* My reproduction of the Samarkand rug detail has been made from a plate in *Oriental Rugs* by W. A. Hawley, published by Dodd, Mead and Company. I am using it by kind permission of the publishers and the family of the author. Photographic reproduction having failed in this case to render the desired detail, I have prepared a wash drawing of it to serve as a substitute. Further illustrations have been borrowed from the following sources: the seventeenth-century German textile from Flemming's *Textile Künste,* published by the Verlag für Kunstwissenschaft, Berlin; the twelfth-century Moorish textile from *L'Art*

Arabe by Prisse D'Avennes, published by Vᵉ A. Morel et Cie, Paris; the Rembrandt portrait of his mother from W. R. Valentiner's *Rembrandt; Wiedergefundene Gemälde,* published by the Deutsche Verlags-Anstalt, Stuttgart.

Finally, my thanks are due to those who have shared the labors involved in the process of publication. Doctor W. D. Howe has lent me constant and kindly assistance on the part of the publishers, and I am indebted to Miss Helen D. Beals for a friendly and diligent reading of the proof and for assistance in preparing the index.

Walter Abell

REPRESENTATION AND FORM

Chapter I

CURRENT VIEWS ON FORM AND SUBJECT–MATTER

Upon no issue is contemporary art criticism more controversial, and in consequence less secure, than in dealing with the relation of "subject-matter" to æsthetic effect. The swing from representation to abstraction, which marked one phase of modern art, carried a corresponding phase of modern criticism with it. The artist, for the most part, has since manifested his creative freedom by making the counter-swing back toward representation, but the critic has not been able to follow the reverse movement so easily. He has been left with the problem of explaining the precise relationship between these two aspects of pictorial and sculptural art and has not, as yet, succeeded in explaining it satisfactorily to all concerned. Widely different views of the matter prevail; views one or another of which certain writers champion strongly and between which others hesitate or waver.

So long as the issue remains an open one, we are not only left uncertain about an important problem of æsthetics, but are basing our criticism upon insecure foundations. Some at least of these views must be wrong and critical evaluations based upon them consequently erroneous. Furthermore, one cannot survey the art of the past two decades without feeling that large numbers of the artists themselves have been swayed by current æsthetic theories as well as by immediate visual inspiration. In many cases, for instance, their creative activities have been influenced by the conception of visual form as ideally abstract and of representation as irrelevant to æsthetic value. If such conceptions are in any degree unfounded, then to that degree these creative activities have been misdirected, with resultant loss to the artist's accomplishment. Hence it becomes important to study the problem of "subject-matter" carefully and, if possible, to bring it to a solution.

In order to recall the points at issue, let us briefly review some of the pronouncements on this problem which have influenced critical thought in recent years. At one extreme, Mr. Clive Bell asserts that subject-matter is entirely unrelated to æsthetic value. "The representative element in a work of art may or may not be harmful: always it is irrelevant. For, to appreciate a work of art we need bring with us nothing from life, no knowledge of its ideas and affairs, no familiarity with its emotions. Art transports us from the world of man's activity to a world of æsthetic exaltation . . ."[1] People who can feel "pure æsthetic emotions . . . as often as not have no idea what the subject of a picture is . . . They are concerned only with lines and colors, their relations and quantities and qualities . . ."[2]—in a word, with what Mr. Bell has attractively termed "Significant Form."

This conception of visual art as abstract in its æsthetic essentials has frequently been supported by reference to the analogy of music. Thus Mr. Sheldon Cheney writes, in his *Primer of Modern Art:* "It is almost impossible to state any theory of the abstract in art without recourse to the terminology and the parallel of music. For music is a wholly non-representative art based in its physical aspect on certain widely understood phenomena. The goal of the abstract painting is

[1] *Art,* p. 25. [2] *Op. cit.,* p. 30.

an art of color as free from associative and objective interest as is this other art of sound. There is no more reason, argue the abstractionists, why painting should be dependent upon the depiction or suggestion of natural objects than there is for music to be dependent upon likeness to natural sounds."[3]

These views concur with the feeling, now almost universally accepted, that no work of art which lacks significant design, or "form," can be æsthetically important, and the equally patent fact that many works—primitive, archaic, and Post-Impressionist—which possess this quality *are* æsthetically important irrespective of the nature of their subjects and of the degree of naturalism with which those subjects are treated. On the other hand, even primitive, archaic, and Post-Impressionistic works are rarely devoid of subject-matter entirely and other schools, throughout the ages, have given it a large place in their work. Purely abstract painting and sculpture is a novelty of our own day, and within our own day has lost its brief ascendancy. Already Cubism is regarded as a necessary and fruitful adventure, a rediscovery and exploration of certain potential elements of art, rather than a complete and permanent form of art in itself. For the most part contemporary artists concur with their predecessors in giving subject-matter an important place in their work.

If subject-matter is "always . . . irrelevant," how are we to explain its persistent presence in the art of all schools and periods? And since subject-matter in one form or another is almost always present, how are we to be sure that it does not play its part in the æsthetic effect which Mr. Bell ascribes exclusively to his abstract "significant form"? Mr. Bell does not provide us with answers to these questions. He is content

[3] P. 159.

to allure and stimulate us with a sweeping intuition and does not attempt to demonstrate its validity with inclusive critical data.

Representatives of the opposite extreme are rare in contemporary criticism. The idea that the æsthetic value of a work of art depends solely upon its subject-matter, axiomatic though it may appear to most laymen, finds no champion from the ranks of those accustomed to critical reflection. But there are many who would give subject-matter an important place in the significance of the work of art, and some who would appear to give it the more important place. Thus for Doctor Herbert Arnaud Reid to be interested "merely in a general arrangement of plastic forms . . . is a strained and unnatural attitude."[4] Surely the artist, in contemplating for example a human face, "has more before him than 'lines, planes and volumes.' Surely, if he is not ridden by theories, he is interested in character."[4] And in discussing the question of what constitutes "greatness" in a work of art, Doctor Reid writes: "I propose in what follows to defend the view that greatness comes from the *content* side of art, and that, roughly, art is great in so far as it is expressive of the great values of life."[5] These values Doctor Reid later describes in terms of "the spectacles of human love, hate, mortality, courage, romance, religious experience, or of the strife of man with himself, or his fellows, or nature"—spectacles which involve "the fulfilments of tendencies which are not only marked and strong, but profound and lofty and broad and far-reaching in the complexity of their implications."[6]

Standard histories of art, though they may advance no thesis, discuss art to a considerable—sometimes to a preponderant—extent in terms of

[4] *A Study in Æsthetics*, p. 321.   [5] *Op. cit.*, p. 225.   [6] *Op. cit.*, pp. 238-9.

its subject-matter and thus, by implication, lend their weight to the view that representational elements are important. *A History of Italian Painting,* by Professor Frank Jewett Mather, may be cited as a well-known example. No work could be richer in translations of pictorial subject-matter into poetic prose. After describing the scene depicted in Giorgione's "Pastoral Concert," for instance—not omitting to evoke for us even the "pleasant, idle sound" of the water which one of the figures is pouring, the author continues with regard to its meaning: "My own reading is merely based on the contrast between the rustic and urban lovers, and an intuition that the courtier in peering so wistfully at the shepherd is merely seeing himself in a former guise. In lassitude, perhaps in satiety, beside a courtly mistress who is absent from him in spirit, there arises the vision of earlier simpler love and of a devoted shepherdess who once piped for him in the shade. The vision rises as his listless hand sweeps the lute strings in a chord unmarked by the far lovelier mistress at the fountain. The golden age of love, like Arcady itself, is ever in the past. Such may be the reading of this poesy. Indeed, all Giorgione's pictures are less facts than apparitions born of roving thought in idleness—such stuff as dreams are made of."[7]

Greater emphasis upon subject-matter than this, it would be difficult to imagine. And in his discussion of the Titian "Entombment" in the Louvre, after contrasting its restraint with Raphael's "sensational version of the same theme," Professor Mather concludes: ". . . perhaps the æsthetic lesson of the picture is that choice feeling is far more difficult of attainment than fine painting."[8] Is all this, in Mr. Bell's phrase, "irrelevant?" Or, as Professor Mather himself must feel, is

[7] P. 381.   [8] P. 404.

"poesy" inherent to the conception, and essential to the value, of these masterpieces?

What Bergson might call the "common sense" answer to these questions—the answer which would recommend itself intuitively to most cultivated observers—is that, whatever the precise relationship between them may be, both form and subject are essential to the significance of most works of art. Such an answer would suggest that we follow a middle course in approaching our problem and this course has been attempted by a number of writers. In one degree or another, the two last quoted, though they may stress the importance of subject-matter, would also recognize the significance of form. We shall draw upon the writings of Doctor Albert C. Barnes for our principal statement of this point of view, and shall also refer again to Doctor Reid in connection with it. Meanwhile let us consider one or two other pronouncements which, if they lead to no critical solution of the problem, lend their weight to the reasonableness of a middle position, and at the same time indicate the difficulty of formulating the principles upon which such a position rests.

Sir Charles Holmes, in his *Grammar of the Arts,* proposes a modification of the abstract "significant form" theory. ". . . since painting appeals primarily to the visual sense, it is perhaps theoretically true that in its purest form it should be entirely devoid of any further source of attraction such as literary, descriptive, or psychological associations provide."[9] In practice, however, this "theory of 'pure' æsthetic" is to be accepted "not as immutable law but as a most valuable working principle . . . we must still think of painting, primarily, as an arrange-

9 P. 112.

ment of beautiful shapes and spaces and colors, but . . . so long as we keep that visual ideal in mind, and give it first place there, we may introduce such psychological, descriptive, or 'literary' elements as the occasion seems to demand—but always at our peril. If these non-æsthetic factors overload or obscure the original æsthetic conception, the result . . . will have gained interest at the expense of pictorial beauty. A transcendent genius, a Leonardo da Vinci or a Rembrandt, may be able to offer sufficient compensation for any such loss. The average painter cannot hope to do so . . ."[10]

Yet in discussing the work of the Paleolithic artist, Sir Charles writes: "So vivid is his mental image that in his picture the quarry often seems to live again. Not only is the general profile lifelike, but the gesture of the head and the action of the legs are those of life itself —the very spirit of the animal is caught as well as its outward semblance . . . in the finest examples the sense of vitality is expressed with so much certainty of hand, and so sure an eye for the refinements of form, that we have to wait for thousands of years before any such potent realism appears again."[11] Certainly in this case the value of the work for the critic would appear to depend largely upon "descriptive" elements, yet if such elements must be taken as "non-æsthetic," how can they contribute value to an æsthetic construction?

The same question might be asked of Messrs. Guillaume and Monro who, in their *Primitive Negro Sculpture,* treat the problem in terms of a "compromise between representation and design,"[12] implying thus that there is a conflict between the two while at the same time both are necessary to the most significant art.

Turning now to the works of Doctor Albert C. Barnes, we find in

[10] *Op. cit.,* p. 114.   [11] *Op. cit.,* p. 12.   [12] P. 133.

them a more positive theoretical basis for the middle position. Even Doctor Barnes, however, begins by recognizing the difficulties of the problem, which he states in the following passage: ". . . the extent . . . to which a picture or symphony may properly also be dramatic or narrative, is one of the most difficult in æsthetics . . . if we say that subject-matter is of no importance, we seem to be committed to an advocacy of purely abstract art, to which representation is wholly irrelevant; and if we say that subject-matter is not irrelevant, then it is not apparent how we shall discriminate between art and mere illustration."[13]

If I rightly gather the central emphasis from the numerous passages in which he touches on the subject, Doctor Barnes lends his support to the view that subject-matter may have a legitimate place in art, and discriminates between its legitimate and its illegitimate use in terms of its relation to the embodying plastic form. "The painter must render his human values in plastic terms; he must make an object or situation move us by its line, color, and indicated spatial relations."[14] "We have subject-matter employed at the lowest level when there is no real plastic equivalent for the narrative or sentimental theme. . . . Even great artists . . . sometimes . . . resort to the illegitimate use of subject-matter. Delacroix . . . was . . . highly romantic and liked to portray fervid emotions. . . . What he felt as heroism and romance, and depicted by exotic subject-matter and exaggerated gestures, seems to us now not sublime but overdramatic, if not bombastic. . . . Tintoretto also painted subjects of a highly dramatic nature, but he gave us the plastic equivalent of the human values intrinsic to the situation, so that while in Delacroix we see flamboyance and melodrama, in Tintoretto we find the peace that æsthetic satisfaction always yields."[15]

[13] *The Art in Painting*, 2d ed., p. 48.   [14] *Op. cit.*, p. 75.   [15] *Op. cit.*, pp. 49–50.

A fusion of subject-matter and form through the use of "plastic equivalents" for "human values" would thus seem to be the fundamental principle to which Doctor Barnes adheres. Establishing a distinction between a legitimate and an illegitimate use of subject-matter, and providing a definite, if somewhat general, criterion of judgment between the two, this principle both clarifies and strengthens the middle position. The many applications which Doctor Barnes makes of it, in discussing the work of specific artists, substantiate its value as a guiding principle in critical analysis. Yet from the point of view of a complete solution of our problem, it leaves unanswered a number of important questions.

How, precisely, shall we define a "plastic equivalent"? Easily grasped in its pragmatic aspect, the conception is not so easy to formulate. Indeed Doctor Barnes writes: "It is impossible to put in words the criterion of plastic embodiment, to give a formula for distinguishing between what is and what is not properly integrated in the visible form of a picture. But a cultivated sensibility will discriminate between the pictorial realization of the values of actual experience, such as we have them in Titian and Giotto, and a recourse to literature such as that of which Delacroix is habitually guilty."[16] This would imply that a precise intellectual grasp of the relation between plastic and representational elements is impossible, yet from the point of view of æsthetics, our problem cannot be regarded as solved until that relation has been determined.

Other questions arise as we pursue Doctor Barnes's discussion of the problem. We are told in certain passages that "relevant judgment or criticism of a picture involves the ability to abstract from the appeal of

[16] *Op. cit.,* p. 75.

the subject-matter, and consider only the plastic means in their adequacy and quality as constituents of plastic form,"[17] and that ". . . of the hundreds of paintings upon detailed analysis of which this book is based, scarcely a score are known by the author in terms of their subject-matter, whether that be, in its general nature, religious, sentimental, dramatic."[18] If complete "abstraction" is made from subject-matter in this way, why are not the plastic qualities, irrespective of "equivalency," the sole ones determining æsthetic value? How, indeed, can the observer be aware of equivalency if he is not aware of the essential nature of the subject-matter to which the plastic elements are equivalent?

Again Doctor Barnes asserts in a number of passages that the nature of the subject is irrelevant to a consideration of æsthetic value in the embodying work. "In that sense, a picture of a massacre and one of a wedding may be of exactly the same type as works of art. We abstract from each the form which is made up of the plastic elements—line, color, space, composition—and determine the quality of that plastic form as an organic, unified fusion of those elements."[19] And we find under a plate juxtaposing Titian's "Entombment" with a Cézanne "Still-life," the comment: "The design of these two paintings is very similar, showing irrelevancy of subject-matter to plastic value."[20] But if two works are plastically similar, yet radically different from each other in subject-matter, it would certainly seem that plastic equivalency could not be found in both of them.

We are obliged also to ask ourselves whether plastic equivalency is the only criterion in terms of which subject-matter need be judged. This seems to be implied in most of the theoretical passages dealing

[17] *Op. cit.,* p. 99.   [18] *Op. cit.,* p. 100.   [19] *Op. cit.,* p. 99.   [20] *Op. cit.,* p. 61.

specifically with the question. Yet in the analysis of actual examples, other considerations are introduced. Delacroix's melodrama seems to be ascribed only in part to failure to provide a suitable plastic equivalent. ". . . exotic subject-matter and exaggerated gesture"—factors involved in the selection and treatment of the subject itself—are also charged against him.

In so far as I can discover, we are also left without a statement of the æsthetic justification of plastic equivalency. Assuming that a work which possesses such equivalency is superior to one which does not, why is this so?

Finally the principle which we are considering, though it provides us with a basis of discrimination between a legitimate and an illegitimate use of subject-matter, leaves unanswered the central question as to whether subject-matter, legitimately used, is or is not essential to the highest æsthetic effect and, if it is, precisely how it becomes a source of æsthetic value and what relation it holds, æsthetically, to form. At least to my reading, it is not clear from the text whether the subject-matter is to be regarded as incidental and subservient to the form, or whether it enriches and completes the form. "In Goya, Daumier, Glackens and Pascin, we find illustration brought to such a high level that it becomes great art. All of them inform us about the situations they portray, but the means used are truly plastic. . . . The pleasure we get from their work is of plastic origin in that the story they tell, while interesting in itself, is entirely subsidiary to the form in which the illustration is embodied. Color, line, space are arranged in forms which move us independently of the comical, ironical or satiric in the situations depicted."[21] This would seem to imply that the significance

[21] *Op. cit.*, p. 50.

of form is independent of subject-matter; that the latter, indeed, when considered æsthetically, can be regarded as negligible.

In another passage, however, we read: "To create an effective design of line and color is something; if the line and color are made instrumental to massiveness, to distance, to movement, that is an important addition; if the dynamic masses in deep space are so composed and interpreted as to render the spirit of the place in landscape, as with Claude or Constable, of religious elevation, as in Giotto, of drama and power, as in Tintoretto, of poignant humanity, as in Rembrandt, the total result attains or approaches the highest summits of artistic achievement."[22] This would seem to imply that form cannot reach its highest achievements unless it incorporates values derived from subject-matter.

If a number of the more general passages already quoted appear to support the first of these implications, the discussions of individual artists more commonly support the second. Cézanne is praised for his power to give "that sense of profound fidelity to the deeper aspects of things, which is the characteristic of all great art."[23] To be sure, Doctor Barnes differentiates such "fidelity" from "photographic imitation" and "literal realism," yet at the same time he recognized its dependence upon "subject-matter that has a sufficient point of contact with the real world to establish relation with our funded experience of real things."

A converse adherence to the same principle is implied in Doctor Barnes's estimate of Matisse. Though "far and away the foremost painter of the day," Matisse "misses the supreme values of painting" because he centers his interest upon "decoration."[24] ". . . he is interested less in objects for what they really are than in the ways in which they can be woven into decorative designs." As a result he "gets

[22] *Op. cit.*, p. 75.   [23] *Op. cit.*, p. 346.   [24] *The Art of Henri Matisse*, p. 210.

nothing at all of Giotto's deep mysticism, and little or nothing of the human dignity of Giotto's figures," nothing of El Greco's "human tension, suffering, and transfiguration," nothing of the "poetry" of Giorgione or the "drama" of Titian or Tintoretto.[25] All this implies that without subject-matter and without the more "expressive" as opposed to the "decorative" treatment of subject-matter, the greatest artistic attainments are impossible.

If, then, the principle of plastic equivalency has value as a guide to critical analysis, it hardly solves the essential æsthetic difficulties of our problem, nor would it seem to permit of an entirely consistent discussion of the sources of æsthetic effect in the works analyzed. If the truth be recognized, it leaves us suspended between abstraction and representation, sensing that both are essential to the highest art, yet uncertain how the seemingly opposite claims of the two can be harmonized. Mr. Cheney, setting reality above the pretense of logic, frankly recognizes this dilemma. "At present," he writes, "the lover of modernist art is in the paradoxical position where he likes the painter who strictly subordinates imitation to a hidden non-representational element, but finds unsatisfying the painter who goes over to non-representation entirely, attempting to create abstract form."[26]

It may be observed incidentally that in a more recent work, *The Art of Henri Matisse,* Doctor Barnes further complicates the issue by advancing his principle of "transferred values." According to this principle, beauty of form is ascribed in part to an expressiveness resulting from resemblances between pictorial designs and natural objects. The designs of Matisse are shown to resemble tapestries, posters, tiles, "flowers and similarly shaped objects, such as conventionalized stars, or

[25] *Op. cit.*, pp. 202–4.   [26] *Op. cit.*, p. 169.

even fireworks. . . ."[27] As a result, the artist "transfers" to his picture the emotional significance resulting from our associations with such objects. From the point of view of abstractionist criticism, this is the extremest heresy. For the combining of plastic elements into form, which the modern critic has been at so much pains to distinguish from the appeal of subject-matter, is here reduced itself to a kind of synthetic subject-matter, one step removed from real objects, but still owing its appeal at least partly to the fact that it suggests those objects and so exploits the expressive capacity which they possess by virtue of our experience with them in life.

Yet why should there be greater æsthetic virtue in evoking our associations with flowers through recourse to a flowerlike pattern, than there is in the more naïve but more direct method of representing the flowers forthright? It is true that in the case of the pattern the expressiveness will emerge transformed as well as transferred; that it will have the appeal of the figurative rather than the literal, and will be strangely impregnated with the separate expressions of the objects that combine to make up the flowerlike design. But it will nevertheless remain expressiveness, and as such will be as distinct as is the appeal of literal subject-matter from the beauty which forms may possess intrinsically, irrespective of their associations.

The middle position finds a further champion in Doctor Herbert Arnaud Reid, whose emphasis on the significance of subject-matter we have already noted. Doctor Reid conceives the successful work of representational art as a "fusion" of subject-matter with incorporating "body-forms"—a conception similar in essentials to that of plastic equivalency. "The ideal for representative art is, that subject-matter

[27] *Op. cit.,* p. 34.

should be as expressively fused with its body-forms as the content of music or architecture is fused with its body."[28]

I shall not quote at length from Doctor Reid's interesting discussion of the subject, as it seems to me to correspond in essentials to that of Doctor Barnes which we have already considered. And if my reading be adequate, it fails of a definitive solution of the problem for essentially the same reasons. I am unable to derive from it a clear conception of how the "fusion" of these two separable aspects of representational art takes place, what precise relation they bear to each other æsthetically, or how "content" can remain such and at the same time be genuinely fused with form. As Croce has indicated, any "content" which has not become form must remain formless, which means that "fusion" has not taken place. If, on the other hand, such fusion has taken place, then all formless material must have been absorbed into the form and no residue of distinguishable "content" can remain.

Although it may not yet have proved a complete solution to our problem, the principle of "equivalency" or "fusion" would doubtless recommend itself to the majority of observers as an advance in the right direction. It is surprising and disquieting, then, to learn that so important a writer as Mr. Roger Fry, after a detailed study of the subject, has come to the express conclusion that genuine "fusion" between psychological and plastic values is difficult if not impossible to attain, and that in consequence one or the other must be subordinated. Following a clue provided by M. Charles Mauron, Mr. Fry suggests[29] an entirely new approach to the problem by making subject-matter, not an extraneous realm of ideas to be imbedded in or "fused" with plastic

---

[28] *Op. cit.*, p. 236.   [29] See his "Some Questions in Esthetics" in *Transformations*.

form, but a potential source of form itself. Like the plastic elements, psychological materials—in the appeal of character, dramatic situation, or other aspects of subject-matter—can be brought into significant relations with each other. When so interrelated they give rise to a form —to a "psychological form"—and this form, as well as its more widely recognized plastic counterpart, may possess æsthetic attributes.

This enunciation of the principle of "psychological form" must have come to many of Mr. Fry's readers, as it did to me, as a fresh and stimulating point of view, fraught with possible answers to long-standing problems. Yet as applied by Mr. Fry to the analysis of works of visual art, it leads to a duality in which plastic and representational elements oppose each other. "Our experiments and inquiries have, then, I hope, given us one result on which we may rely with some confidence: the notion that pictures in which representation subserves poetical or dramatic ends are not simple works of art, but are in fact cases of the mixture of two distinct and separate arts; that such pictures imply the mixture of the art of illustration and the art of plastic volumes. . . ."[30] Each of these "arts" may have its proper form, but the relation between the two is one of "tension" rather than affinity. The greater the plastic interest, the more subordinate must be the psychological one if conflict is to be avoided, and *vice versa.*

"Psychological form," therefore, would seem to be closely related to what most of the critics previously quoted have referred to as "mere illustration" and have objected to precisely because of its separation from its embodying plastic foundations. It explains, by reference to potential beauty of form, the appeal which a "literary" construction may have for us, but it only confronts us with new problems in our

[30] *Op. cit.,* p. 27.

attempt to deal with visual art involving both plastic and representational elements. Or more accurately, it carries us back to our original problem of trying to determine the relationship between these two sources of effect, which are at once so constantly associated with each other in art and so difficult to harmonize in æsthetic theory.

In summary of this introductory review, we may say that there exist in modern critical writing at least three mutually incompatible points of view with regard to the problem before us: that subject-matter has no æsthetic significance; that subject-matter may have at least a bearing upon æsthetic significance if successfully fused with an equivalent plastic form; and that subject-matter may have æsthetic significance through a "psychological form" of its own, but that this cannot be successfully fused with a significant plastic form. Each of these views seems to have certain points in its favor, yet at the same time, if the questions raised above with regard to them be well taken, none can be accepted as a final solution of our problem. Nor has any one of them as yet succeeded in eliminating the other two; the conflict between them remains unresolved.

Further study of the problem, therefore, seems necessary. Such study is attempted in the following pages and will lead us to a fourth view of the problem in terms of which it is possible, I believe, to resolve the differences between the three existing theories and at the same time to answer the subservient questions to which they give rise.

In the earlier parts of our investigation, the reader will be asked to analyze his visual experience in some detail, a task not to be accomplished without resort to some degree of intellectual effort. Theories proposed on the basis of general reflection or intuitive insight, untrammelled by the more exacting demands of critical analysis, usually afford pleasanter reading. The trouble with such theories is, that although they may stir the imagination by their freshness or by the illumination which they bring to certain phases of experience, they rarely provide a final answer to problems so intricate as that which we are now considering. By proceeding as nearly as possible in a scientific temper, by examining as closely as possible all relevant data before we attempt to formulate any theories, we shall at least have assurance that our eventual conclusions lie as near the truth as we are capable of pressing.

CHAPTER II

ÆSTHETIC PREMISES

The theory of æsthetics in which our argument finds its point of departure has been elaborated by George Santayana in his work, *The Sense of Beauty*. According to this theory, æsthetic values fall into three general classes described as the beauties of material, of form, and of expression. Beauties of material are those qualities of matter, such as the glowing freshness of a color or the purity of a musical tone, which afford agreeable sensations and which are thus described as possessing "sensuous charm."

Beauties of form are those which result from an ordering of parts or elements into significant relationships, as does the rhythm of interwoven lines in an arabesque or the symmetry of towers grouped in a façade. Since form is one of the chief terms of our problem, we shall return to it at greater length in a moment.

Beauties of expression result from the workings of association as one of the mental processes involved in our activity of contemplation. That activity does not—cannot—confine itself exclusively to the sensations and perceptions stimulated by the immediate objects of attention. ". . . the human consciousness is not a perfectly clear mirror. . . . We not only construct visible unities and recognizable types, but remain aware of their affinities to what is not at the time perceived; that is, we find in them a certain tendency and quality, not original to them, a meaning and a tone, which upon investigation we shall see to have been the proper characteristics of other objects and feelings, associated with them once in our experience. The hushed reverberations of these associated feelings continue in the brain, and by modifying our present reaction, colour the image upon which our attention is fixed."[1] As a result, the present image becomes "expressive" for us of meanings or states of feeling which it could not awaken in us had we no dormant store of them to be awakened. Such is the case when we feel that the construction of a Gothic cathedral is "daring," that its vertical lines embody "religious aspiration," or that its shadowy spaces with their smouldering walls of glass exhale a "meditative calm" and "mystical exaltation."

It must, of course, be recognized, as Santayana is careful to state,[2] that the results of association are by no means all æsthetic. The cathedral may turn our thoughts to memories or dreams of travel, to medieval history or Christian purpose, to questions of style or authorship. In such cases, the associated ideas or suggested problems replace the intrinsic beauties of the present object in our attention, and our experience, so far as concerns that object, ceases to be æsthetic. But if the states of consciousness awakened by association are not so much precise ideas as diffused meanings and feelings, they may remain an integral part of the immediate experience. They will then be "objectified" as expressive qualities of the object under contemplation. Such is the case with the qualities ascribed above to the Gothic cathedral; such also with the "reserve and dignity" of the Greek temple, the "deep solemnity" of Byzantine mosaics, the "lyric joy" of Renoir's paintings, and with a thousand other moods or meanings, some of which are a

[1] Pp. 192-3.
[2] For his discussion of the distinction between æsthetic and non-æsthetic association see pp. 193-5.

factor in our enjoyment of almost every work of art. In all such cases, we are attributing to inanimate objects qualities of experience which are possible only to living beings, yet so spontaneous is the process of attribution and so directly inspired by the nature of the object before us that these qualities seem as much a part of its existence as do its beauties of substance or of form.

We shall start, then, from the premise that æsthetic values are potential to material, to form, and to expression—psychologically stated, that they may arise from the experience of sensation, of perception, or of association— and that, presumably, all æsthetic values are reducible to one or another of these three categories of effect. This, of course, does not imply that these three categories are necessarily equal in the importance of their contributions to the beauty of art.

Our specific problem of form and representation can best be approached by determining, as nearly as possible, the exact nature of these two factors with which we are about to deal. A statement of the nature of form is provided by Santayana[3] and the sense he gives to the term has, in essentials, become an axiom of modern æsthetics. In this sense, "form" may be defined as any whole produced by organized relationships of elements or parts. Specific types of relationship give rise to specific formal effects; to component aspects of form. Repetition with regard to a central point or axis produces symmetry; ordered relationships of size give rise to proportion; relations involving ordered movement result in rhythm; and similarly with other principles of organization such as emphasis and harmony. In any given object, these individual effects of relations, which present form in its simplest

[3] *Op. cit.* Part III, particularly pp. 82–97.

manifestations, become component elements of larger wholes. They are interwoven with each other in a more extensive network of relations, a network which at length embraces all the elements present in the object, and all their component combinations, and so gives rise to the total effect of that object as a whole. This embracing network of relations, which gives the object its identity, constitutes the complete "form" of that object.

It will be observed that this sense of the term "form" is obviously more inclusive than a number of others also current, and must be distinguished particularly from that which would limit form to tangible shape or body. In the latter sense form has sometimes been opposed to color, Florentine painting being praised for the one, Venetian for the other. Form is then conceived chiefly in terms of linear design and of third-dimensional weight, volume, and solidity. Such effects are properly considered formal, since they are an outcome of certain correlations of line, surface, and light. But they are formal, not because they involve delineation or solidity, but because they result from relations. Such relations do not stop with the definition of solid bodies nor are they in any sense peculiar to such bodies. Color in turn becomes an element of form when it is worked into significant relationships. Those Renaissance painters who explored its resources (their number included Florentines as well as Venetians) were not abandoning the quest for form but were pursuing it into new and subtler spheres. Through color they were able to extend and vary the total network of visual relations which their work embodied. As a result, their form became richer and more complete than it could have been without this development.

Thus while form can be created in tangible materials, it need not be, and is itself in fact never tangible. The form of a statue is not its solid substance but the relationship of parts which produces a given total effect in, and in relation to, that substance. Conversely forms can be created from combinations of intangible elements, as literary and musical forms, mathematical forms and "forms of government" all witness. And it is this wider and more philosophical sense of the term which may be etymologically the most accurate, for the word is believed by some philologists to derive from a Sanskrit root meaning "law, system, order." Form is, then, that "law, system, or order" in accordance with which individual elements or parts are brought into significant relationships with each other.

These facts are all well known and widely accepted and I have presumed to review them here only because they offer the chief contribution of accepted knowledge toward the solution of the problem at hand. For use at a later stage in our discussion, let us reserve two principles emphasized in the foregoing summary: first, that form is in essence a series of organized relations; and, secondly, that relations do not pre-suppose any given characteristics, such as plasticity or tangibility, in the related elements, but may exist between any elements whatsoever.

Let us turn now to consider the second factor in our problem, that of "subject-matter" or "representation." It has received much less study from modern æstheticians and critics than has form; has indeed, as we know, been excluded by some of them from the sphere of æsthetic consideration. Hence it can hardly be dealt with in summary fashion. We are here concerned, not with established conclusions, but with a field for investigation.

It is apparent at the outset that if our premised classification of æsthetic values was adequate, subject-matter, as such, cannot constitute an æsthetic value. For we recognized that the three classes of æsthetic values were those of material, form, and expression. This classification admits form at once to an accepted place in the scheme of things æsthetic. But there is no class, "Beauties of Subject-matter." Thus far the abstractionists would seem to have the right of the controversy, for we recognize that form may possess intrinsic æsthetic value and we cannot claim a similar standing for representation.

We should be far from justified, however, in assuming that because such is the case, representation is necessarily unrelated to æsthetic values. Its status in this respect is no different from that of the plastic elements. There is no class, "Beauties of Plasticity." Colors and lines are not intrinsically æsthetic—they may be ugly as well as beautiful. They affect æsthetic values only in so far as they become contributory to beauties of material, of form, or of expression, subserving them in the relation of means to end. Yet the modern critic has not, for this reason, seen fit to exclude them from æsthetic consideration. On the contrary, he has found that their contributory function entitles them to serious study and analysis. Since plastic elements, not in themselves æsthetic, are thus found to be significant in their contributions to æsthetic effect, it is not illogical to suppose that representational elements might do likewise. We have certainly encountered no proof as yet that their relation to æsthetic values is negative or even neutral.

It will be useful for our study to analyze representation as closely as possible and to determine how it is related to the types of æsthetic value which we have recognized and to the chief other potential sources of such value, namely the plastic ones. Conversely, we must determine what effect is produced upon the æsthetic value of visual forms if representation is completely excluded from them. In order to investigate these and related problems, let us begin by reducing visual experience to its simplest elements and then progressively trace its development into higher and more complex states. Four such states or "strata" of vision will appear in the course of our analysis, each one built upon that which precedes it, the final stratum carrying us back to the fullness of visual reality. In each stratum we shall seek to observe what æsthetic effects are there possible, what the relation of these effects is to form and to representation, and what relation these two terms of our problem seem to bear to each other.

Chapter III

ABSTRACT PLASTIC FORM

The simplest state to which we can reduce vision is that of a continuous field of undifferentiated color. We should be observing such a field, or at least a convenient approximation to one, if we fixed our attention upon an evenly tinted wall or an expanse of clear blue sky. Under such conditions the only element in consciousness—apart from mere extension, a form hardly significant enough to attract attention to itself—is that of a single visual sensation: the sensation afforded by the given color. The individual color, then, may be taken as affording the most rudimentary source of visual experience and, for that reason, as constituting our first stratum of vision.

In order to study the effects potential to this stratum, I have performed an experiment which the reader, if he wishes, can easily repeat for himself. It consists in isolating various colors, and observing each of them in turn with attention to the content of the resulting experience. Failing more elaborate apparatus, a set of colored papers of the type prepared to illustrate the theory of color will suffice to provide the requisite materials. I employed a set of this kind; a set in which each of the twelve hues recognized in the Prang theory of color was represented by five variations of value and intensity, giving in all an assortment of sixty colors. Each color occupied a separate sheet of paper large enough to fill the central area of the field of vision when held at reading distance from the eye.

Placing selected sheets before me one by one, I contemplated each of them long enough to experience, and introspectively to examine, all the reactions which it seemed capable of affording me. Apart from the factual identification of the color before me, I found that my responses were of three different types and that any single color might stimulate any one, any two, or all three of them. These responses, as I experienced them in a few typical cases, may be tabulated as follows:

IDENTITY OF COLOR CONTEMPLATED	RESULTING RESPONSES		
	1 *Sensation Characterized by:*	2 *Impression of:*	3 *Suggestion of:*
Dark purple.......	....	dignity	....
Pale blue-green....	exquisite delicacy	lyric joy; feminine quality	sea-foam; twilight sky
Rather bright yellow-green.......	....	spiritual or passionate intensity	spring grass and buds under the sun
Bright golden yellow...........	"richness"	physical well-being	gold; sunflowers
Warm gray-brown.	grateful, soothing effect	peace, restfulness; forgetfulness of care	winter leaves; fields before grass has sprouted in spring
Bright red........	vividness	warmth	flames
Orange-rose......	lusciousness	....	certain roses

A first group of responses, listed in Column 1, corresponds to the immediate quality of each individual color sensation, a quality which is felt to be delicate, "rich," soothing, intense, or of some other nature. When enjoyable, as in these instances, each of these qualities affords the observer an experience of sensuous charm or beauty of material. But the various sensations, delicate, intense, or other, do not usually stop as such. They seek out associations in the dim storerooms of subconsciousness, evoking moods or meanings originally experienced in quite other contexts. Thus they assume a power of *expression,* introducing "dignity," "feminine quality," and other associated effects like those listed in the second column. In some cases, they do even more. As indicated in Column 3, the associative process continues and focuses itself in the definition of particular objects or classes of objects— usually those which most commonly embody the given color in nature. Then blue-green evokes the thought of sea-foam, bright red of flames.

Thus we observe that even so simple an element as a single color may not only possess sensuous charm, but may also give rise to expressive effects, and may further suggest specific objects with which it has frequently been associated. It will be noted that in this latter respect, it verges closely on representation. It introduces an embryonic and half-formed subject-matter even where no intentional representation has been practiced and no precise subject-matter is actually present. We shall return to this fact shortly. Meanwhile we may note that, with regard to meanings, a color appears from the above experiment to occupy a position midway between a musical tone and a word. It is often more definite in meaning than a tone; it is usually less definite in meaning than a word. It may remain a pure sensation at one extreme; at the other it may be nearly as rich in meaning as the equivalent word—say flame—but it does not inevitably call attention to that meaning as does the word.

It is obvious that a single color, however rich in sensuous charm, does not provide a sufficient basis for the creation of a work of art. A piece of undifferentiated material can, it is true, be deeply moving in its beauty; can indeed constitute the chief source of æsthetic value in certain objects where the form is elementary. The smouldering blue of certain Persian potteries is a more unique achievement than any other element involved in the incorporating work, at least if that work is undistinguished in shape or decorative pattern.

Even here, however, we have to qualify in a double sense the æsthetic significance which we attribute to the color in its purely sensuous aspect. Seen on a bowl or vase, the color is not undifferentiated but involves a range of values and intensities corresponding to the range of light and shadow which accompanies a three-dimensional object. What we contemplate, therefore, is not a single color but a series of related colors harmonized by the persistence through them of a common hue. Our enjoyment is due only in part to sensuous appeal; it involves as well a perception of harmony. Thus it carries us out of the sphere of material into that of relations or *form*.

Furthermore, even in its joint significance of material and form, the beauty of the color is never the sole factor in determining the æsthetic value of the incorporating object. Qualities of structural design will also affect our judgment of that object as a whole, and there may be other elements involved. Were its color the only respect in which the piece was æsthetically satisfactory, we should be obliged to consider it defective as a work of art.

The stimulus to individual sensation, then, remains potential material for inclusion in works of art, rather than a sufficient basis for their existence. Artistically our first stratum of vision is a substratum. Additional elements must be provided before artistic creation becomes possible, and to encounter such elements we must leave the sphere of the individual sensation and enter a second stratum. This we do if we replace our uniform color-field by one within which we recognize a juxtaposition of two or more distinguishable colors. Such a variegated field might be approximated by laying papers of different colors one beside the other, by changing the plain wall for a geometrically patterned one, or observing the natural world through a piece of ground glass which permitted us to perceive only flat color areas on a surface.

The relationship of one color to another now becomes a factor in our experience. In addition, the several colors may constitute divisions of the field having recognizable boundaries. Lines and shapes will then appear within the variegated surface. Since these elements, shape in particular, introduce determinate units which may be compared with each other, size likewise enters consciousness at this point. So also may movement, for the shapes—as in the case of moving objects seen upon our ground glass or that of "color-music"—may be animated, changing their position in the field of vision. Furthermore, even when a shape or line is itself stationary, perception of it will usually require movement on the part of our eyes, and such movement we objectify and feel as a quality of the object—as when we attribute flow of line to a painting or a building.

It is evident that our second stratum introduces no new classes of sensation, but rather brings together sensations each of which could have been experienced separately in the first stratum. This being the case, it provides no new sources of sensuous charm, and indeed there are no such sources available. Pure visual sensation reduces itself inevitably to the stimulus of the single color. The new factors which enter to enlarge our experience in this stratum result from the joint presence of several differentiated elements and from the perception of some interrelationship between them. We have, in other words, entered the realm of form; not necessarily æsthetic form, since the relations may not be so organized as to satisfy the sense of beauty, but form in its general psychological sense, since without some combination of elements, some perception of related parts in a common field, we should still be at the level of undifferentiated sensation and would not have entered our second stratum at all.

Taking now a few examples of the types of relationship which we encounter in this new stratum and proceeding as before, we arrive at very similar results, except that our first column is now occupied by effects of form instead of by those of material. Characteristic examples are as follows:

IDENTITY OF FORM CONTEMPLATED	RESULTING RESPONSES		
	1 *Perception Involving Sense of:*	2 *Impression of:*	3 *Suggestion of:*
A color combination: bright red and green	contrast tempered by harmony	gaiety, vivacity	. . . .
————	. . . .	steadiness, repose	the horizon; a long sure flight; a road seen from above
╲	. . . .	instability	slope of a hill; something falling or sliding
∿	rhythm	suppleness; freedom from constraint	waves
▭	symmetry and proportion	dignity, formality	a window; a framed picture

Again we have certain immediate effects, now those of perception rather than sensation; of form instead of material (Col. 1). Again these immediate effects stir associations, awakening in us the consciousness of certain bodily, mental, or emotional states which may easily merge with the perceived data to become beauties of expression (Col. 2). In all the above cases, the associations also recall particular objects of past experience, thus displaying an impulse toward the formation of subject-matter (Col. 3).

Exploration of the effects potential to our second stratum leads readily to one conclusion, namely, that even at this level, the æsthetic resources exploitable through form are vastly richer than those potential to material alone. We now have color, line, shape, size, and movement as "means" to employ in creating beauty. The "ends" to which we can employ them are almost infinite in variety and often lofty in potential effect, including all the resources of harmony, contrast, balance, proportion, rhythm, and emphasis, in so far as these can be developed in abstract forms upon a flat field. It is obvious that even in one of its several possible sets of relations—that of harmony for instance—color alone can achieve effects far richer than those resulting from the sensuous charm of the individual color, however striking that charm may be.

Thus in potential contributions to beauty, form appears at this level to take the dominant place. Nor are its contributions exclusively "formal" in character. It enormously multiplies the resources of expression, for each new combination of elements will stir its own new associations and work toward individual expressive effects. Furthermore, form may have a retroactive effect upon the materials from which it is built, for elements in combination modify each other and by so doing may enhance their original sensuous qualities. Brightness of color, for example, will be heightened if the color affording it is brought into contrast with others markedly different in hue or lower in intensity.

We shall not be straying from the main path of our argument if we pause for a moment at this point to consider the relation of form to the sensuous materials from which, in the first instance, it is constructed. It has been said that art-forms are distinguished from purely intellectual constructions, like those of mathematics, by the fact that in art the significant relations are embodied in sensuously pleasing materials. This would make it seem that any advantage in æsthetic effect which art may hold over mathematics results from the fact that it supplements the beauty of form, common to both, by a beauty of material distinctive to it alone.

But the mathematical form, when written down or printed, is also embodied in sensuous materials and these materials, in the case of a finely wrought manuscript or a beautifully printed page, may be so refined as to possess æsthetic value. It is true that the range of sensuous effects is not likely to be so extended even on the beautifully printed page as it is, say, on the surface of a painting. But the real crux of the matter, the essential distinction between the mathematical and the art-forms, results from the fact that in the former, the sensuous materials establish no essential relation to the formal significance. It is hardly conceivable that one equation would gain value by being printed in dark green ink on light green paper, while another would produce its full effect only if printed in blue ink on yellow paper. The material and the form, though each may possess æsthetic appeal, remain detached from each other. The form does not absorb the sensations;

hence the form itself remains to that extent a limited one. There are relations present—those between the material and the form—which remain external to the formal significance.

In art, such is not the case. The colors employed are more than mere physical embodiments of the design. The light and dark green, the blue and yellow, become an integral part of the design itself. They are interwoven, not only with each other, but also with the other elements present, in such a way as to form an inseparable part of the governing context of relations. As a result, all the elements involved are merged in the unity of that context. No phase of what is perceived remains external to the significance of the perception.

Conversely, the range of elements united in that perception is extended and enriched: the form achieves an amplitude which would not otherwise be available to it. For in addition to the relations between its component formal elements—its lines and shapes and movements and quantities—it also involves relations between its embodying sensuous qualities, and between its formal *and* its sensuous qualities. The materials present, over and above any intrinsic sensuous charm which they may possess, perform their major æsthetic function by increasing the number of potential relations and so augmenting the possible beauty of form.

And in any given case, if the highest æsthetic effect is to be achieved, the materials employed must subserve the quality of the form which embraces them. However charming in their purely sensuous aspect, they will be inappropriate to the given context if they fail to take their places in the network of relations which constitutes the governing form. Once more we observe that form emerges as the dominant source of æsthetic values, but at the same time that maximum formal significance demands the assimilation by the form of pre-formal or sub-formal qualities.

It is in this second stratum—that of a vari-colored surface incorporating lines and shapes—that we meet the simplest creations of visual art: the two-dimensional patterns familiar to us in certain types of rugs, textiles, ceramic decorations, and elsewhere. These patterns may be either "abstract," that is geometrical, or they may be representational, employing motifs based upon, and suggestive of, the forms of flowers, human figures, and other objects. It will serve our purpose best to exclude representational pattern from our consideration for the time being and to concentrate our attention on geometrical effects. By so doing we shall be able to pursue our study of form untroubled by considerations of subject-matter and can determine what degree of æsthetic significance is potential to visual form without recourse to representation. We shall then be better able to judge, in our subsequent observations, whether representation adds anything essential to visual art or whether visual form is equally significant without it.

Of the two varieties of pattern potential to our present stratum, we shall, then, consider for the moment only the first: that which is abstract or geometrical. Such pattern holds a high place in the esteem of the lover of visual art both for the inherent beauty which it may possess and for the ideal position which it seems to occupy in presenting visual form in its simplest and purest embodiment, unadulterated by considerations of subject-matter. Yet if one examines a wide range of decorative art with such pattern under consideration, one is likely to qualify one's initial enthusiasm for geometrical ornament by a number of reservations.

The pattern is almost never attempted as a source of independent effect, but is employed in a decorative capacity upon objects having other and often more significant sources of appeal. The appropriateness of the given pattern to the shape of the given object might still be considered as an extension of form within the present stratum, if the object were a rug or a wall surface and thus two-dimensional. But often the form of the object is three-dimensional, as in pottery, and introduces sources of effect beyond those which we have yet recognized. Similarly, the beauty of that form usually depends in part upon appropriate use of the medium and fitness to function—expressive considerations which become associated with our experience only as we acquire a knowledge of the capacities of materials and the functions to be fulfilled. Thus beauty of pattern is usually only one element in the total beauty of a patterned object.

Furthermore, if we consider the whole range of decorative art, we find that geometrical pattern has been relatively little used. Most decorative pattern is of the representational, and not of the abstract, variety. Why this is so we begin to surmise if we limit ourselves for a considerable period of time to the contemplation of purely geometrical pattern.

In the first place the formal resources of purely geometrical pattern appear to be limited and, in comparison with those offered by other forms of art, relatively mechanical. A pattern like that reproduced in Fig. 1 is delightful in its first effect upon us. But that effect pales with continued contemplation, nor can it easily be renewed by turning from one example to another. We soon become aware of a similarity between examples and of a restriction of them all to one limited sphere of effect. Great as may be the beauty of geometrical pattern, it does not, even at its best, provide forms of sufficient richness to prove permanently and exclusively satisfying. It leaves the observer with his craving for beauty still partly unsatisfied—with an urge toward more complete æsthetic fulfilment; an intuition of effects not here attained and not attainable in this type of form.

And indeed we know historically that those schools of ornament which give a dominant place to geometrical design have usually been forced to do so by external interference. Thus the Mohammedan emphasis upon abstract ornament is a natural consequence of a religious injunction against the use of human and animal forms. Even in this case, the adherence to abstraction is not complete. The decorator makes free use of floral motifs, which do not share the ban, and not infrequently evades the restriction which the church has sought to impose upon him with regard to more extended representation.

If the designer, thinking to escape the limitations suggested above, attempts greater freedom and complexity than is possible to geometrical pattern, yet still does not wish to introduce representation, a new difficulty meets him. It may be illustrated by Fig. 2. The abstract but informal shapes used in this pattern transgress the bounds of obviously geometrical, hence patently inanimate, forms. Their freedom gives them a suggestion of life, yet they refuse to identify themselves with any living things known to us. Our minds hover on the verge of seeing them as natural forms, yet are unable to do so. Perplexity results and we feel ourselves impelled, either to return to purely geometrical pattern on the one hand, or to cross over to clear representation on the other. It is doubtless in order to avoid such confusion that most pattern falls rather sharply into one or the other of these two classes. Only in exceptional cases does the designer merge their characteristics in such a way as to create disturbing intermediate effects like that of our example.

One other fact concerning geometrical pattern remains to be noted. Contemplate the pattern of Fig. 1 continuously for several minutes. If your experience is similar to mine, you will find that after a certain length of time you are unable to attend longer to its purely geometrical relations and that representational images begin spontaneously to appear in it. In my own case, these include lighted windows in a dark wall, totem-pole faces, human figures grouped two by two. The same process of association focusing itself in the suggestion of specific objects, which we have already noted in observing simpler elements, again manifests itself, but with one important difference.

Simple and relatively indeterminate elements, like individual colors or lines, are completely malleable to associative interpretation. Whatever suggestion of objects they lead to, appears so natural to them and at the same time may increase their appeal so considerably, that it affects us as a pleasant amplification of their significance. But the more complex and determinate a form becomes, the more definite the geometrical relations which it involves, the less readily does it respond to representational interpretation. As just noted in the case of our lace pattern, representational images are certain to be suggested by it if our attention is held long upon it, but these images are now restricted by the geometrical forms of the pattern. As a result they are likely to seem but forced and inadequate suggestions of the things they represent, and at the same time to assume a character, humorous or grotesque, which is out of harmony with the dignified beauty of the geometrical pattern. The unity of the form suffers from the apparition within it of these discordant elements. At the same time, the psycho-

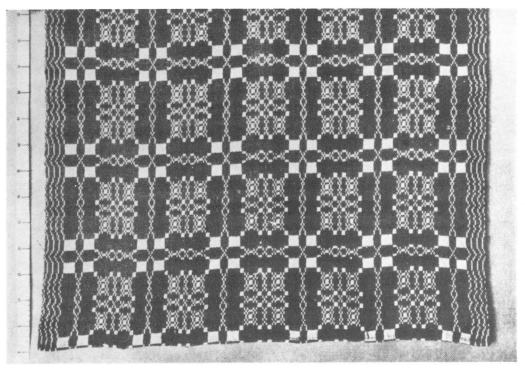

FIG. 1. SEVENTEENTH CENTURY GERMAN TEXTILE
(After Flemming, *Textile Künste*)

FIG. 2. SAMARKAND RUG (DETAIL)
(After Hawley, *Oriental Rugs*)

logical impulse which gave rise to them is not adequately fulfilled in them, but is left dissatisfied and gropes for more complete expression.

This self-asserting representational tendency which we have met at each of the levels of vision thus far considered, a tendency which manifests itself even in our contemplation of non-representational objects, suggests a fact important for an understanding of our problem. Visual elements appear to be so inextricably linked in our minds with the objects of the outer world that it is psychologically impossible for us to attend to them long in abstract form. To attempt to do so is to repress a phase of our spontaneous mental functioning which resists repression. It tends to express itself even when there is no adequate ground for its expression and, if it meets resistance, imposes upon us a certain sense of strain and frustration. Visually at least, the mind appears to be a representational instrument. However much, at certain moments, it may delight in abstract form, it cannot long subsist on the rarefied atmosphere of abstraction.

In this respect, it will be noted that the stimuli received through sight and hearing are opposite in character. Whereas the former cannot easily be kept abstract, the latter cannot easily be made representational. Sounds are never conceived by us as *parts* of real objects. They are thought of, at best, as produced *by* such objects. Songs are sung *by* birds; they do not seem to us parts of the birds themselves, as do the colors of their plumage or the shape of their bodies. Most of the sounds used in art—in language and in music—have not even this external association with natural objects. If a definite meaning is ascribed to them, it is largely by agreement upon an arbitrary intellectual convention. There is not in most words any inherent key to their meaning. The proof is that we cannot understand a language unless we laboriously familiarize ourselves with the meanings assigned to its words. Other meanings might have been given, and in fact the same word in different languages often has different meanings.

Music presents a converse illustration of the same principle. Its natural state is abstract. If, in the composer's experience, it comes to be associated with particular objects or ideas, he cannot transmit those meanings to us with any degree of precision through the music itself, but must have recourse to an external explanation of his intentions— to a "program." And if we do not receive a copy of this program, or do not care to read it, the music will either remain for us diffuse in its emotional suggestions or will find, in *our* experience, contexts of meaning quite different from those assigned to it by the composer. Thus while colors and lines continually resist abstraction and force themselves into connection with objects, sounds resist connection with objects and revert at the least opportunity to an independent abstract existence. These considerations might awaken doubts as to the truth of the traditional dictum that music, as the art of "pure form," sets a model toward which the visual arts should strive. Since the foundations of these two artistic worlds are radically different from each other, since the mental tendencies which they start lead in opposite directions, we might rather suppose that they should seek opposite goals. We shall return to this question later.

In summary of our second stratum of vision, we may say that its æsthetic resources include varied colors, with their correspondingly varied qualities of sensuous charm (a charm sometimes intensified by the interaction of one color upon another) and that to these beauties of material are now added opportunities for the creation of many and varied beauties of form in geometrical pattern. But when made the object of exclusive attention, such pattern proves to be restricted in its formal possibilities and at the same time fails to satisfy an insistent representational tendency of our minds and ends by subjecting that tendency to dissatisfaction. If æsthetic demands are fully to be satisfied, ways must be found of further developing and enriching visual form; and if mental equilibrium is to be maintained, opportunity must be afforded for an expression of the representational impulse which is started, it would seem, by practically all visual impressions.

In order to find resources for the further enrichment of visual form we must enter a higher stratum of vision; one in which an increased number of elements will be available for formal construction. Such a stratum—the third in our sequence—may be defined in terms of mass, space, and the other "plastic" elements which lie beyond the borders of our first two strata.

Psychologically, the key to this third stratum—the factor which distinguishes it from those previously considered—would seem to lie in the fact that the elements upon which it depends for its existence are not received as direct visual sensations, but demand the interpretation of visual stimuli in terms of non-visual experience. In its psychological aspect, our first stratum corresponds to the single visual sensation, our second to the concurrence of varied sensations and the perception of relationships between them. Projected on the retina, the web of sensations giving rise to vision forms a mosaic of colors, lines, and shapes, flatly disposed, and thus corresponds in essentials to the variegated color-field in terms of which we have defined our second stratum. Presumably immediate visual impressions, uninterrupted by attendant meanings, can assume no more developed form than this. They *indi-*

cate additional elements, but we cannot learn what they indicate, we cannot become aware that they indicate anything, through the exercise of sight alone.

Through other phases of our experience, however,—our movements about the world, our encounters with solid bodies, our exploration of their surfaces by means of touch—we become advised of physical properties not originally seen. So, as children, reaching for the moon but finding it always beyond our grasp, we become aware of distance. Next we discover that certain variations of color, line, and size to be detected by the eye, are due to the existence of this newly experienced aspect of reality. Henceforward we interpret such variations in terms of the distance to which they correspond. We have learned to "see" distance. By the same process, our vision becomes sensitive to other elements not previously perceived and the visual world expands for us accordingly.

As already implied, the most striking features of this new stratum result from the introduction of the third dimension. The flat surface to which we have hitherto been limited fades away like a curtain before a stage, allowing our gaze to plunge into a world of three dimensions. Mass and space, with numerous attendant qualities, make their appearance. Volume, solidity, and weight emerge as potential attributes of form, which was previously flat. Surfaces other than that of our original flat color-field appear—the varied surfaces of the objects in our new three-dimensional world: some flat, some curved, some broken by folds or other irregularities.

Illumination also becomes, for the first time, a distinguishable fact and a potential source of effect. Previously, since it fell undivided upon a flat surface, it could have affected us only as a constituent of color values and intensities and would not have appeared to us as an element separable from color. But now, falling against three-dimensional bodies and broken by them into the infinite range of light and shadow, it becomes in itself an important element of vision.

Texture likewise reaches visual maturity in this stratum. Physically, a limited range of fine textures would of course be possible on the surface of our second-stratum color-field. Coarser textures would involve an appreciable degree of depth or third-dimensional quality and a play of illumination over the resulting surface irregularities, neither of which are possible in that stratum. And from the psychological point of view, even those textures which were physically potential to the second stratum, could hardly be felt as such within its limits. To a second-stratum consciousness, that is to one uninformed by other than purely visual impressions, they would appear merely as fine interminglings of lighter and darker color. They would hold no tactile suggestiveness. Only when associated with the experience of touch, are they recognized to be the signs of varied textures. Thus associated, different interminglings can be read as indications of roughness, smoothness, softness, and other qualities of which we first become conscious through tactile sensations.

The many new elements thus encountered in our third stratum enrich the repertoire of æsthetic effects in a number of ways. The development of texture reinforces our first stratum with a new battery of sensuous qualities. The caressing depth of velvet, the sheen of silk, the softness of down, not to speak of a hundred other sensuous effects of texture, now become available for visual suggestion. Each constitutes a potential beauty of material. But we should note that these new "materials" are not actually such in vision—not actual sources of visual sensations. They merely appear as such through association.

How devious are the mental ways by which our impressions arise and how little we are usually conscious of their precise nature, may be seen by analysis of the manner in which such an element as texture becomes for vision a source of sensuous pleasure. It reaches the eye only as sensations of two or more closely related colors. These occur in a particular form—they are perceived in relation to each other as a certain type of intermingling. This intermingling is then interpreted by association to indicate a given texture. This texture in turn awakens further associations, including those which have been established with it through tactile sensations. The enjoyment of these sensations, expressively evoked, then becomes a potential source of æsthetic experience. Thus actual sensations, related in a form and interpreted through association, become a means of suggesting other sensations not at the moment actually experienced. The whole circuit of mental activity—from sensation through form to expression and so back to sensation—is involved in the mere perception of such a quality as the softness of a velvety texture.

Apart from its contribution to sensuous appeal, expressiveness, as such, gains new resources in the present stratum. The varied textures not only have their suggested beauty of material; they bring with them overtones of meaning. Rich textures become symbolical of cultural refinement and material ease; hard, coarse, or barren ones suggest phases of life which are crude, ascetic, or impoverished. Light and shadow reveal affinities to the whole range of man's emotional life, from the sinister forebodings that lurk in darkness to the mystical assurance which makes radiant light a symbol of spiritual transfiguration. Space implies freedom, air to breathe, and opportunity for movement. Mass evokes overtones of strength, permanence, inertia, pressure or resistance, thrust and counter-thrust.

But most significant of all is the new variety and amplitude which is now possible to visual form. Composed in three dimensions, instead of two, the number of its geometrical relations, the complexity of its geometrical forms, is greatly increased. Furthermore—a point of great importance to our argument—many of the additional sensuous and expressive elements enumerated in the two preceding paragraphs are not limited to a purely sensuous or expressive significance. They present themselves as additional elements that can be employed in building form; they enormously increase the number of possible relations into which visual elements and their emanations can be brought. Not only do we pass beyond the limit of flat shapes on a surface into the world of three-dimensional shapes standing free in space. If a given solid shape—say a cylinder—exists in stone and is perceived to be the support of a certain superstructure, then considerations of weight and resistance enter our contemplation of it and influence our judgment of its form. What proportions will appear most satisfactory in it, is no longer a matter of simple geometry. It is a matter of geometry plus engineering. Tension merges with dimension and moulds the form to satisfy a more intricate and exacting series of relations. Form and expression interplay with each other to produce a richer and more complex form. The form absorbs the expression and is, at the same time, partly determined by it.

A large part of the plastic or physical beauty of nature would emerge into the consciousness of one who contemplated the world from this stratum of vision. In the realm of art, we should expect the typical development to be that of an abstract three-dimensional plastic form. The geometrical patterns of our second stratum, released into the world of mass, space, illumination, and texture, might be expected to expand into more complex geometrical designs, different from their second-stratum prototypes only in that they involved additional plastic elements, including an additional dimension.

In point of fact, there appear to be no art forms which are three-dimensional equivalents of geometrical pattern. Abstract or purely geometrical forms in three dimensions do not seem to exist. The forms of architecture, and of industrial arts like pottery, are frequently conceived to be such. They are obviously non-representational, but are nevertheless far from being "abstract" in the complete sense in which geometrical pattern is so. Purely abstract form, of which such pattern is the type, is self-determined by intrinsic considerations of design. Architectural and industrial forms, on the other hand, are not so determined. Clay has never been moulded nor stone piled to satisfy an exclusive interest in solid shapes or grouped masses and spaces. Indeed the ceramic sphere or the granite pile in which we could discover none but a geometrical significance would appear to us eccentricities.

As already implied in our reference to the cylindrical support, the forms of architecture and the industrial arts are inspired and conditioned by factors not intrinsically formal or æsthetic—chiefly by the requirements of certain utilitarian functions. Plastic design interacts with extra-plastic forces and is moulded into a fabric of relations in which these forces play an influential part in determining the final nature of the form. An exact classification of the several species of form, therefore, would require that the type which we are now considering be separated, not only from representational form, on the one hand, but also from abstract form on the other. It constitutes a distinct type by itself; a type which might be designated "functional" form. And if it has a kinship to abstract form in being non-representational, it also has a kinship to representational form in being modified by extra-plastic forces. These forces in fact influence it in manner closely parallel to that in which subject-matter influences form in sculpture and painting. Thus the distinction commonly drawn between architecture and the representational arts is only partially justified by fact, and if architectural form seems to present an exception to the principles which we are now about to consider, that exception is apparent rather than real.

Since architectural and industrial forms are not representational, however, a full consideration of them would lead us aside from our immediate study of form and representation. Having noted that they involve factors not given in our present stratum of purely plastic elements, and that they are not therefore to be accepted as examples of third-stratum form, we must dismiss them from further consideration and turn our attention to the only three-dimensional arts remaining for investigation, namely painting and sculpture. Do these arts present us with forms of the type for which we are looking: forms which remain abstract and which at the same time exploit the increased plastic resources of our present stratum?

Only in work of one category, produced during approximately two decades by a comparatively small number of artists, can we find anything approaching non-representational, three-dimensional form. This is the work done by the Cubists and other modern exponents of so-called "abstract" design. Figs. 3–6 may serve us as examples. Such work was the outcome of a concentration upon plastic form so complete that representation became for the artist a matter of indifference. Here, if anywhere, we might expect to find formal beauty of a high order.

Formal beauty such works certainly possess. At their best—let us say as in Fig. 4—they possess it to a degree beyond the possibilities of geometrical pattern. Exact repetition of motif gives way to a freer and subtler principle of organization. Modulation and development play a larger part in the form, which gains accordingly both in the number and the variety of its component relationships. To minds oppressed by the formlessness of Salon pictures, this reassertion of the significance of plastic form came with refreshing vigor, like air from windows just thrown open in a room that had long been unused. Yet when contemplated exhaustively and compared in its formal achievements with significant art of other types, such work reveals limitations similar to those already encountered in abstract two-dimensional pattern.

In the first place, the form is still limited in the number and complexity of its component relations. It is not what we might call ultimate in its formal beauty. One has but to recall the orchestrations of Titian and El Greco, of Renoir and Cézanne, to realize that they afford a richness and subtlety of perceptive experience, a massiveness of formal impact, not to be derived from these abstract creations. Though the latter are capable of affording pleasure, they are not capable of exhausting it. There are still further extensions of form, wider and deeper networks of relations, which the mind feels its capacity to grasp and toward the experience of which an intuitive desire impels it.

In the second place, forms of this type, when considered in large numbers, reveal less variety and individuality than would usually be

FIG. 3. PICASSO. ABSTRACTION
(Courtesy Valentine Gallery)

FIG. 4. PICASSO. WOMAN WITH MANDOLIN
(After Einstein, *Kunst des 20. Jahrh.*)

FIG. 5. PICASSO. THE POET
(After Einstein, *Kunst des 20. Jahrh.*)

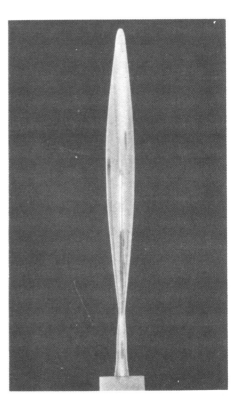

FIG. 6. BRANCUSI. BIRD
Museum of Modern Art, New York. (Sunami)

found in a similar range of representational art. Apparently the field for creative development and for personal expression offered to the artist by abstract form is a restricted one. Or, to state the same fact in its subjective aspect, the production of abstract form is apparently a strenuous and exhausting operation. It appears to be difficult for the human mind to create visual forms which are purely, or even largely, its own invention. It may be fascinated by the problem, but after a period of interesting and instructive experiment, it is likely to find continued progress difficult and to give up the attempt. Its capacity lies in forming or ordering motifs presented to it from external sources rather than in conceiving abstract motifs of its own.

We might reduce the same observation to more general terms by saying that the mind can mould experience to its purpose, but cannot, of its own resources, *generate* experience. As Professor Dewey has convincingly shown,[1] experience arises only from an interaction between *two* factors, of which the mind constitutes but one: a sensitive agent and its environment. Now the environment of human sensitivity is the natural universe in which it lives and by which it is itself continually in the process of being moulded. To exclude that universe from art is to disqualify for artistic uses all but a minor and artificially segregated aspect of the artist's experience. It is accordingly to deprive him of his chief sources both of material and of creative stimulus. Under such conditions, it is but natural that his work should prove difficult and that his product should be limited in the range of its effects.

Finally, these forms confront us inescapably once more with problems allied to representation. In very few cases are they abstract in any

[1] See his *Art as Experience*, pp. 13–19. The idea is restated in other passages throughout the book, providing the point of departure for its principal developments.

but the relative sense suggested by their difference from traditional representation. And this difference, though sufficiently strong to dominate our perceptions at first glance, proves upon examination to be one of degree rather than of kind. In most part, these works are no more pure abstractions than Impressionistic works are pure impressions. In calling them "abstractions," if we accept the term as anything but a convenient label, we allow the generalization carried by a word to press beyond the status of the forms themselves. In point of fact, the larger number of them are modified representations, inspired by real objects or, if not, then unintentionally suggesting them, and in either case modifying our experience by the presence of a representational element.

If, as in Fig. 3, this element is very slight, the observer will probably have difficulty in deciding whether the artist's purpose was abstract or representational; or—if the purpose be accepted as representational—in determining the precise significance of the representation. The work then imposes a mental confusion similar to that noted in the case of informal but abstract pattern. In the larger number of so-called "abstract" forms, as in Fig. 4, the representational content is sufficiently definite to be unmistakable in intention and character. We are no longer dealing with genuinely abstract form. However simplified or modified the representation may be, it is representation nevertheless, and carries art forward to a type of form beyond the limits of our present stratum.

Furthermore, we should note that even when painting and sculpture do approximate to an abstract state, they rarely if ever provide examples of the type of form for which we have been seeking. In Figs. 5 and 6, we have designs in which any representational element is so slight as to be negligible. But instead of providing us with examples of third-stratum abstract form, these works at once gravitate to other spheres of effect. The painting impresses us primarily as a decorative pattern, and thus reverts in essentials to a second-stratum type of form. The sculpture identifies itself in the mind with forms of the architectural or industrial type. This polished metal shape evokes the processes of machine production, the fitness to purpose (be it of vase or torpedo), which are characteristics of functional art. Beyond the limits of our second stratum—beyond the sphere of surface pattern—it seems to be impossible for the mind to conceive a truly abstract object: an object the organization of which is determined by no external purpose or meaning. If unable to interpret a form in terms of any representational meaning, it automatically turns to the only other relevant sphere of meanings known to it: the functional.

In short, "abstract" painting and sculpture elude classification within the boundaries of third-stratum form. Either they fall below it, remaining at the level of our second stratum, or else they press beyond it into associated spheres of meaning, representational or functional. In so doing, they furnish further evidence for the statement made above that genuinely abstract form in three dimensions does not exist. If any of the types of form which we have just examined may be considered as an authentic third-stratum form, it is that which vacillates uncertainly between the second stratum and the fourth; that which we have found to be dissatisfying because of the mental confusion which it imposes. Artistically our third stratum seems to be a kind of vacuum, or perhaps we should say a storm center, from which forms are thrown off toward adjacent territories and within which they cannot exist in a state of equilibrium.

Two complementary facts meet us at the point which our discussion has now reached—the dividing point between abstraction and representation. On the other hand, as we have observed above, forms constructed of third-stratum elements usually involve some degree of representation, even when the artist was absorbed in building abstract relations and would willingly have dispensed with representation altogether. Representation seems to spring up spontaneously at this point, like wild grain in the fields, even though no one prepares the soil for it or cares to reap the harvest.

Equally striking is the converse fact that although our present stratum is rich in potential æsthetic values, as indicated by our initial discussion of it, only a few of these values are exploited to any large degree in the abstract or semi-abstract forms which we have been considering. Though many textures are now perceivable, most of them are not directly creatable in painting or sculpture. Only the textures of the physically present materials are available so long as the form remains abstract. An artist like Giorgione can *represent* velvet, and so enrich his painting with its suggested sensuous charm; he cannot manipulate paint in such a way as actually to give it that charm.

So with distance and the opportunities which it brings for varied groupings of parts in space. Hardly available to sculpture as an æsthetic element under any conditions, space becomes available to painting only through representation. And though all space is by nature abstract in one sense, for that very reason it is at the same time real. Space cannot be introduced into a picture without appearing as real space; in effect as well as in the process of its creation, it is representational. It is perhaps for this reason that the Cubist painters, who were perhaps the most radical exponents of abstraction, confined themselves so largely to two dimensions and experimented so little with the goupings of abstract elements in space. In the literal sense of the term, their work is less "cubistic" than "squaristic."

Similar considerations apply to effects of illumination, mass, and the surfaces or planes which masses embody. Only through representation do any of these elements become potential to painting. In sculpture, mass and surface, being physically present, constitute exceptions to the present rule, and by so doing indicate that whether a given element is actual or representational in a given work of art depends first of all upon the characteristics of the medium employed.

In summary of the preceding discussion, we may say, first, that when third stratum elements are combined into a form at all, that form tends almost automatically to become representational; and secondly, that if the artist seeks to limit this representation, he deprives his work of the larger number of third-stratum plastic possibilities, forcing it in the direction, either of second-stratum pattern or of functional form. Why the forces underlying the development and perception of form should operate in this manner, we shall consider in our next chapter.

We have now traced visual form to the maximum development which it can attain in decorative design, sculpture, and painting without becoming definitely representational. We have found that even at this level it draws upon the expression of extra-visual experience for many of its effects, that from the point of view of purely formal beauty it cannot be regarded as ultimate, and that it appears to be incapable of restraining itself within the bounds of abstraction, but breaks across those bounds into the realm of an elementary representation. We have also found that in proportion as it resists this representational tendency, it limits the range of its own plastic possibilities; and that if it succeeds in remaining approximately abstract, it has the further disadvantage of frustrating one phase of the mental activity involved in contemplation and so fails to afford the observer an experience of complete satisfaction.

It would be at these limits that the arts under consideration would stop were representation definitely debarred to them, and it is evident that even from the point of view of purely formal beauty, most, if not all, of the true masterpieces of sculpture and painting lie outside these limits. In fact, if critical analysis were insufficient to prove the limitations of abstract visual form, the history of art would offer strong grounds to support its contentions. The fact that so few artists in the long career of art have attempted to create such form is in itself significant. The further fact that those twentieth-century artists to whom the idea of so doing came as a fresh inspiration—artists whose chief concern was the creation of formal beauty—turned back from the attempt after a few short years of experiment, is conclusive evidence that the ore they found in this new vein. was quickly exhausted. We cannot assume that they returned to representational art because they had lost their interest in form. Rather was it the case that representation proved necessary to the continued pursuit of their interest in form.

If the preceding analysis is accepted as accurate, it becomes evident that our problem takes on a somewhat different aspect from that which it may originally have held in our minds. The question is no longer whether representation in sculpture and painting is desirable; we have seen that without it even the highest *formal* effects are impossible. We have in fact resolved the "paradox" involved in the position of those modernists who find themselves little better satisfied with abstract design than they were with imitative naturalism. We have seen that abstraction fails to provide full æsthetic satisfaction for essentially the same reason that "mere illustration" does, namely that it limits form. If naturalism overlooks the principle of organized relations, abstraction limits the number and variety of the elements between which relations can be organized. The result is the same in its effect on formal significance. Hence those concerned with such significance are justified in avoiding the one as well as the other. Their paradoxical wavering between the two reduces itself to a deeper logic, intuitively sensed in experience even when it had not become articulate in theory.

The inconsistency of what we earlier called the "middle position" lay in the assumption that abstract form constituted ideal or maximum form, hence that maximum form led away from representation. In point of fact, as we have discovered, maximum form demands the concurrence of representation. In thus indicating a fundamental link between form and representation, our investigations are leading us toward that same middle position, but they are also providing that position with new, and I believe more logical, foundation.

The further questions that now present themselves might be stated as follows: what new sources of enrichment does representation bring to form, and what is the precise relationship between these two constituents of the work of art, both of which seem essential to the highest artistic achievements? In search of answers to these questions, let us next analyze representation as we did abstract form, returning to our first stratum of vision to trace its development from its simplest manifestations.

CHAPTER IV

PLASTIC GAINS THROUGH REPRESENTATION

We have already noted that single colors and lines may start associations which focus in the suggestion of definite objects, a certain red suggesting flame or a horizontal line the horizon. This object-suggesting power possessed even by isolated visual elements is the sub-soil from which representation springs. Representation in the complete sense, however, hardly appears at so rudimentary a level. The suggestion of objects remains too vague and general, allowing for variation in the experience of different observers.

But now suppose that the color suggesting flame is brought into conjunction with lines also suggesting flame. The two suggestions concur and together crystallize into a definition. The composite suggestion of flame becomes fixed and inevitable, common to the experience of all observers, and we say that this combination of color and line stands for, or "represents," a flame. The form created by the inter-relation of the two component elements, while still retaining all the qualities which it would have possessed as an abstraction, takes on an additional significance which renders it representational. Representation, then, is an outcome of the associative suggestions started by practically all visual elements. It becomes a definite factor in visual experience at the point at which there is a sufficient number of concurring suggestions to mould the observer's response into the identification of a given object.

On the basis of these facts, we can readily understand the spontaneous emergence of representation in third-stratum forms which we noted above, together with the plastic limitations imposed upon such forms by abstraction. It is obvious that the more visual elements we bring together, the more force of object-suggestion we generate. It is obvious also that third-stratum vision necessarily involves a considerable number of elements. We do not enter the third stratum at all unless to color, line, shape, and size (our second-stratum elements), we add some additional effects of distance, volume, illumination, or texture. We have thus brought together practically all the plastic elements of visual reality. Such an inclusive combination of elements generates a veritable flood of object-suggestions. Some of these suggestions inevitably concur and representation is born whether we will or not. Conversely, the only way to resist this conquest of form by representation is to restrict the number of plastic elements and thus to prevent any strong confluence of object-suggesting associations.

Hence it follows, as we have already seen, that the artist who seeks to cultivate abstraction in our third stratum, labors under a double handicap. He finds it almost impossible to keep his forms abstract; he sacrifices many plastic possibilities in his attempt to do so. Abstraction, like the fabled white elephant, becomes for him a troublesome charge, continually breaking through the bounds provided for it and at the same time devouring a good portion of its master's creative resources. Small wonder, then, that the majority of modern artists have found their abstract period a difficult one to prolong and have willingly returned to one degree or another of representation!

Representation becomes potential to art at the level of our second stratum, where color, line, and shape can be used in combination to suggest particular objects. We find them so used in decorative design when we turn from geometrical to representational pattern of the type illustrated in Fig. 7. Lines and shapes are no longer solely geometrical, but become terms for defining the figures of peacocks with small animals at their feet, with tree-like forms between them, and with pairs of small birds beneath the bases upon which they stand.

Taken by and large, as we study its effects in any considerable range of decorative art, the representational element thus introduced into design would seem to increase the possibilities of æsthetic effect in a number of different ways. In the first place it makes possible an increased significance of the form from the purely abstract point of view. The confusion between the abstract and the real, which made it difficult to employ free shapes in abstract ornament, no longer obtains, since the shapes are now definitely identified with real objects. There results an immense increase in the number of motifs available for design and a corresponding economy of the creative effort involved in designing. Instead of being forced to invent motifs upon which to compose, the designer now finds them flooding upon him from every corner of a million-motifed universe. The infinite variety of forms presented or suggested to him by nature, forms impressed upon his mind since childhood through daily contacts with his natural environment, stand ready for his use—materials not only waiting, but pressing, to be employed. Instead of having to engender seeds, he finds them in abundance ready to be sown and can devote himself to their cultivation; to the more congenial and at the same time more productive task of developing his nuclear motifs and combining them into higher orders of form.

The stimulus thus presented by nature not only offers a ready start-

FIG. 7. TWELFTH CENTURY MOORISH TEXTILE
St. Sernin, Toulouse. (After Prisse d'Avennes, *L'Art Arabe*)

FIG. 8. CÉZANNE. MT. STE. VICTOIRE
Barnes Foundation, Merion, Pa. (Morgan)

ing point for design, a source of inexhaustible inspiration; it also promotes excellence in the resulting creation. In their elusive freedom and unending variety, natural motifs confront the designer with difficulties which lead to fresh study and new discoveries. They cannot easily be handled in terms of the simpler geometrical relations, which settle quickly into formulas. The problems of relationship are more complex, the form to which they give rise when solved, accordingly, more varied and intriguing. Thus representational pattern is likely to surpass geometrical pattern even in respect to purely geometrical relations. Considered solely on the abstract plane of colors, lines, and shapes combined in decorative patterns, representation results in a potential enrichment of *form*.

Extended into our third stratum (that of the third dimension, illumination, and varied textures) the corresponding enrichment of plastic form is possible to an even larger degree. Sculpture gains little so far as new elements are concerned, for its power of *representing* plastic qualities is limited, and those plastic elements which it physically possesses, it had already employed in building "abstract" forms of the type considered in our preceding section. But pictorial form gains enormously. Mass, space, light and shadow, unlimited variety of texture—all those plastic elements denied to abstract pictorial form, since none of them can be physically introduced into pictures—these elements and their numerous derivatives can now be evoked for contemplation and given a seeming reality in the work of art by the magic of representation. And even in the case of elements previously available, such as color and line, the penetrating study of nature induced by representation leads to a range and subtlety of effect that would never be attained by the artist whose interest was confined to artistic abstractions.

In all these ways, the number of elements to be related in the form is immeasurably increased, the network of relations grows correspondingly wider and more intricate, and the form, once more amplified, now has available to it a potential richness of effect which is capable of satisfying prolonged contemplation. At this level of third-stratum vision assimilated into art through representation, plastic form has available to it, for the first time, the resources essential to the achievement of its maximum fullness and beauty.

The art-forms which most fully exploit these resources—or rather the forms which exploit them and at the same time most fully exclude still other sources of effect that we shall next consider—are those of landscape and still life treated primarily for their plastic values. We may take as our example a landscape by Cézanne (Fig. 8). The plastic form of such a work is obviously richer than that of any of the others which we have yet considered, and for the reasons which we have just noted.

We are thus led to a first conclusion concerning representation, namely that it provides important resources for the enrichment of plastic form. Even in its abstract aspect, representational art is, on the whole, much richer in form than abstract art. We have not yet reached the plane of subject-matter in its most typical and, to its adversaries, most objectionable form: that in which "literary" elements are introduced through the representation of life forces such as character and action. Possibly the advocates of abstraction will feel that thus far we have merely confirmed their case by demonstrating that plastic form is the only essential source of æsthetic concern, since we have considered representation only as means of promoting such form.

So much in fact is true. But we have also shown that representation is not, as they frequently assume and have sometimes expressly stated, a force running counter to form—one between which and formal values a "compromise" must be effected, or even one which is completely unrelated ("irrelevant") to formal beauty. On the contrary it promotes, is indeed indispensable to the achievement of, the highest formal beauty. It provides for the growth of artistic forms a process of assimilation similar to that which enables higher forms of life to evolve by absorbing the virtues of lower ones. It enables the representational arts to assimilate, from natural objects and from works of minor art, an infinite variety of plastic qualities which otherwise they could never possess. Without it, as we have already seen, the growth of visual form is arrested at a rudimentary and relatively insignificant level.

A further and secondary conclusion derives from this first one, namely that plastic form and abstract form are by no means identical, as they are frequently assumed to be. Elementary plastic form *may* be abstract, as in the case of geometrical pattern. Highly organized plastic form, at least in painting, is *never* abstract. It is always representational; always dependent upon elements which become available to it only through recourse to representation. Plastic and representational elements, therefore, are not to be thought of as clearly separable from each other. They are closely interdependent. Were their respective territories represented graphically, the overlapping areas would be much larger than the mutually exclusive ones.

Chapter V

ÆSTHETIC EFFECTS IN ULTRA–PLASTIC
REPRESENTATION

We are now ready to consider the effects possible in a fourth and last stratum of vision, that in which representation goes beyond the enrichment of plastic form to develop subject-matter in its own right, subject-matter which is interesting for non-plastic or "literary" reasons. Forms are no longer contemplated exclusively in their plastic aspect. Mayhap they become peacocks with adumbrations of bird life hovering about them; with overtones of the vital or spiritual traits of character—vigor, a touch of haughty pride, a touch also of self-assertion and combativeness. Mayhap they become more than peacocks—children and men and women, devils and saints and deities.

Let us recall the mental steps by which it becomes possible for lifeless stone or pigment to conjure up these living entities with all their intangible workings of mind and spirit. Color affords a series of differentiated visual sensations. These sensations occur in relationship to each other, giving rise to a perception of form. Certain associations stirred by elements of this form concur in their object-suggesting expressiveness and awaken images of recognizable objects. These images, identified in the mind with the objects themselves, now stimulate a new range of associations, evoking the residuum of experience gained through contact with such objects in life.

It is this new deposit of associations which constitutes our fourth stratum. Its range is immense, its variety and subtlety extraordinary, its power of moving us profound. In the light of meaning with which it bathes plastic phenomena, the landscape ceases to be detached mass and space and becomes an aspect of the world we live in, where fields are ploughed and houses inhabited, where mountains are climbed up strenuous paths and have swift breathing at their crests; where suns rise and set and there is a different mood at dawn from that of dusk. So the still-life becomes flowers of a kind we have picked, or pots and pans of a kind that hang in our kitchens or in kitchens under brown tile roofs in Provence. So the shape which has become for us the representation of a human form goes on, as such, to arouse perceptions and responses of a hundred kinds which life has woven for us around humanity. We may feel the freshness of child life or the mellowness of age, we may admire the vitality of physical health or mental vigor, we may read the workings of the incorporeal personality that animates the corporal frame, reacting to an *infanta's* shy reserve, an unscrupulous pope's cunning, or a saint's spiritual radiance. Echo beyond echo, world beyond world, the reverberations prolong themselves, like footfalls ringing through a shadowy nave. Almost the whole range of life, with its suffering and its ecstasy, its quick sensitiveness of nerve and soul, its groping upward and its stumbling back, seems to be accessible to the silent couriers of association sent out by visual stimuli; couriers so swift that their movement is imperceptible, so skilled that their service is unrecognized.

Involved in lesser degree in representational decorative design like that of our peacocks, in increasing measure in third-stratum plastic creations like our Cézanne landscape, these new meanings, when definitely exploited, produce the avowedly representational art which constitutes the most characteristic product of painting and sculpture as it also embraces by far the larger portion of their output. From paleolithic animal drawings to ballet scenes by Degas, from the kings and gods of Egypt's dawning millennium to the acrobats of Picasso or the heroes of Mestrovic, this consciously representational art stretches in unending sequence, its herded mammoths succeeded by Panathenaic processions and they by Annunciations and Crucifixions and they by the revels of banqueting societies and so on without end.

What, now, is the effect upon æsthetic values of this incorporation into art of ultra-plastic representation? Vaguely and somewhat remotely, in the penumbra of consciousness, there appears to be first of all an accretion of sensuous charm. New sensations or, to be exact, expressive reverberations of them, enter the domain of art. If my own experience be typical, they are chiefly tactile in origin. Hearing, taste, and smell, each of which has accumulated for the mind an individual reservoir of sensory impressions, seem to respond little to visual stimulus. A picture of flowers does not often suggest perfume to me, nor one of fruit, the pleasures of the palate; neither does one of birds or musical instruments recall the vibration of sound upon the ear. Or if they do, the suggestion stops with ideas. I may *think* of smell, taste, or hearing; I am not likely to feel any of the sensations which an actual stirring of them would involve. Hence there results no addition to my immediate sensuous experience.

But with the sense of touch it is otherwise. Visual and tactile experiences seem to be linked with a closeness which permits visual stimuli, through association, to become expressive of tactile sensations. In contemplating a nude by Rubens I may seem to feel—not merely think about—the warmth and softness of opulent human flesh. Similarly before a Renoir flower piece, I may feel the coolness of dew-laden petals. And before a Cézanne landscape, I may feel a firm resilient earth beneath my tread; an exhilaratingly clear atmosphere in my lungs. Not feel these things, of course, with the sensuous amplitude of actual physical contact, but feel the feeling of them as it has been deposited in my mind and is awakened by association; feel an echo of sensation which is in itself an obscure stirring of sense and which enriches with new overtones the sensuous experience involved in my contemplation of the work before me. And since these overtones may become for me a source of additional value in that act of contemplation, they are potentially a source of additional æsthetic value in the object contemplated.

Nor is this increase in sensuous charm, this enrichment of "material," the only type of expressiveness resulting from the associations introduced into the work of art by subject-matter. Our commerce with things is not limited to the sensations they afford us. Landscape, in the thousand dealings we have had with it in life, has come to mean more to us than ground upon which to tread and air to breathe. It may mean, as it meant to Poussin and Claude, a grandeur reminiscent of ancient glory, or as it meant to Corot, a mood of lyric tranquillity and mystical communion with nature, or as it must have meant to Cézanne, a sensing of the immutable laws that govern the atoms in their spheres and hold the mountains at their eternal stations.

The human figure cannot affect us exclusively as flesh to caress. We know that a spirit inhabits it and that this spirit has its metal and its moods. *Character* inevitably attracts our contemplation. So does *action,* when character meets character in the harmonies or conflicts of existence—when Giotto brings Joachim to the sheepfold or Rubens sets the nymphs and satyrs at Bacchanalian revels. Our stores of "funded experience" are vast; there are few reaches of existence from which they have not garnered some tribute. The "hushed reverberations" of almost all that life means to us may steal forth from the shadowy crypts of subconsciousness, stirred by the influence of subject-matter upon the mind; steal forth to mingle with our perception of the images which that subject-matter presents and to endear those images to us.

Nor is the expressiveness which they hold for us purely a matter of personal associations, external to the work of art. The artist's experience of life was as full as our own. The images he embodied in his art emerged from, and were moulded by, that fullness. And so, by the meeting of his treatment of subject-matter and our own funded experience of life, our experience of representational art becomes potentially charged with "human values" which could exist neither if the work were abstract nor if our past were abstract; values which are the expressiveness of life embodied in images of life and its world.

It goes without saying, as the abstractionists have insisted, that the associations stirred by subject-matter will include many of a non-æsthetic character: many which are capable of carrying us away from the intrinsic qualities of the work of art to personal reveries or other irrelevant activity. The "Mt. Ste. Victoire" may remind us of Provence; its hotels, the condition of its roads, the experiences we have had there on one occasion or another. The "Mars and Venus" may set us dreaming of the Mars or Venus we hope will one day be ours or turn our thoughts homeward to the one that is. In such cases, the association is too distinct to be lost in the experience of contemplation which stimulated it. But only a failure in discrimination could lead one to assume that because this is sometimes so, it is necessarily always so. That would be to exclude expressiveness from æsthetic consideration altogether. Then we should not be justified even in calling Michelangelo's line "forceful" or Titian's color "restrained." We could not longer refer to the Ravenna Mosaics as "dignified" and we should have to patronize the *naïveté* which led Beethoven to misname a symphony "Heroica."

I have already referred, in my introductory review of the types of æsthetic value, to the distinction between æsthetic and non-æsthetic expression[1]; the distinction between associations which merge with the qualities of the object under contemplation and those which remain separable from it. If a more detailed statement of this distinction is desired, it will be found in Santayana at the passage to which reference has already been given. Suffice it for our present purpose, to assert that no association is by nature inherently "irrelevant" to the experience of art, provided it fuses with the other phases of that experience and so becomes an integral part of it. The expressiveness of subject-matter is no exception to this rule. The deep significance of character, the spiritual mellowness and resignation, which a Rembrandt study like Fig. 9 expresses for us, are not irrelevant to Rembrandt's work nor even separable from it. We cannot contemplate that work at all without contemplating them as an intrinsic phase of it. And they are a phase which it can embody only through its subject-matter and to which we can respond only through associations that prepare us to find that subject-matter expressive.

[1] See pp. 20–21.

Yet it can readily be admitted that a painting or a statue may possess expressive subject-matter and remain comparatively insignificant as a work of art, and that he misses much—in fact most—of the value of great works of representational art who responds only to the expressiveness of their subjects. Indeed, as the novice soon discovers, he who goes to them solely preoccupied with their expression is likely to be satisfied only by certain limited types of work: only by an avowed realism or by what, to more cultivated observers, appears a sentimental idealism. Most representational art, the Michelangelo sibyl as well as the Matisse odalisque, vexes and mystifies him by the liberties which the artist has taken with natural forms. If such ungainly or "distorted" work is expressive for him at all, it is likely to express abnormality in the subject, waywardness or incompetence on the part of the artist, or some other negative element. In the light of these facts it might seem that the expressiveness of subject-matter, even if it be admitted to æsthetic standing, is nevertheless an element of slight importance to art.

In order to judge the point, let us summarize our findings thus far with special reference to the relative significance of the three categories of æsthetic effects. By far the greatest contribution to beauty, as we have traced the development of the latter in art, must be ascribed to form, a source of effect which we have seen amplified in successive strata until, in the last, it reached a potentiality of profound impressiveness. This dominant formal beauty has, in most cases, been supplemented by an accompanying experience of sensuous charm and of expressive meaning, but these experiences, however delightful, have always remained secondary. A form of even moderate amplitude, such as a geometrical pattern, can afford us a considerable experience of beauty and will readily be granted the status of art, even though it may possess little beauty of material or expression. But the converse cannot be maintained. A sensation alone, even of the most luscious Venetian red; an expressive evocation alone, even of Mars or Venus, remains a *phase* of experience rather than an experience complete in itself. No art has ever attempted to limit itself to sensation or expression alone and none which did so could mean much more to us than sundaes or souvenirs. And when all three sources of appeal are combined in a work of any significance, it is always the form which dominates. Thrilling as may be the glow of color in a Cézanne landscape, inviting as may be its picture of a clear and spacious world, these pale in significance beside the inexhaustible beauty of its governing form. Is ultra-plastic representation at best, then, merely an adjunct to an adjunct; a factor contributory to beauties of material and expression which are themselves secondary in importance to the beauty of form?

Not so, for we have yet to speak of its chief contribution to beauty— and in doing so we reach the heart of our argument. This contribution lies in a potential enrichment and final amplification of that dominant source of æsthetic values, the beauty of form. If the preceding analysis has served any purpose, it has prepared us for the discovery of this relation between form and representation by breaking down a number of widely accepted but imperfect conceptions both of form and of representation, and of the part that each plays in æsthetic effect. We have found, in the first place, that the three accepted classes of æsthetic values are not derived from mutually exclusive compartments of experience, as even Santayana might seem to imply through his limitation of a given element like color to a single phase of his discussion, that of beauty of material. Such a compartmental view of æsthetic effects could be diagrammed as follows:

Beauty of material   — — — — — — — Immediate visual sensation: color.

Beauty of form   — — — — — — — — — Arrangement of elements in tangible shapes or bodies possessing such characteristics as symmetry and proportion.

Beauty of expression   — — — — — — — — In art, subject-matter appealing to ultra-visual interests and producing such effects as the dramatic, tragic, or humorous.

But such a view gives only a very imperfect conception of psychological reality. As we have seen, sensuous charm is modified by the retroactive effect of form on materials and enlarged by the suggestion of sensations through expression. Form is not a department of effect exclusive of material and expression; it is not exclusively form of form, as are the tangible shapes built up of lines and surfaces already formal in themselves. It may exist in the relation between indeterminate sensuous elements, as in the harmony between two colors. It may work out to establish relations with expression, as architectural form is modified by extra-visual considerations of "program" and structural fun ion. Expression does not wait to begin its stirrings until a subject-matter is represented for it. It may be awakened by a single color, as is a mood of dignity by dark red or purple; or by a form, as that same dignity may be evoked by a grouping of parts in formal balance. Thus there is a crossing and recrossing between every phase of our experience; each builds up, and at the same time is built up by, the others. The contemplating mind is a fluid organism. Its responses, started in part by separate processes, meet and oscillate against each other, mingling in a common movement, like waters in a shaken bowl. More accurately diagrammed, our experience would be somewhat as follows:

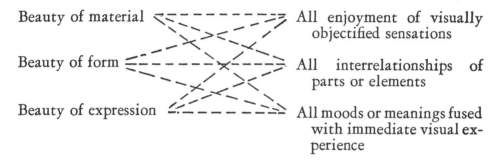

It is into this fluid interaction of elements that the expressive phases of consciousness resulting from subject-matter are poured; phases of consciousness which bring with them hundreds, nay thousands, of new elements of thought and feeling. And in the revolution of the mental turbine, it would be impossible for them to keep their identity exclusively as expression. They are churned with the swirling currents and used for all the power which they are capable of generating. We have already noted that they generate some stirring of sensation to enhance the beauty of material. Most important of all, they present themselves as thousandfold new elements to be woven into the form.

Form, the organizing force which gives all elements their respective places in a governing network of relations; form which we have watched progressively extending its domain from the rudimentary ordering of points in a line or lines in a rectangle to the heroic conquest of a whole plastic world in a Cézanne landscape; form which, like a vessel flooded by successive waves, has no sooner been immersed in new aspects of experience than it begins to rise through them and eventually emerges once more at the top—form now begins its organizing work upon the expressive elements injected into it by representation and once again may end, not only by maintaining its sovereignty but by extending that sovereignty over new domains. For, as we have repeatedly observed, form is not limited to relationship between tangible elements, nor does it presuppose any given type of element whatsoever. Form is an order or organization, and the degree of order, the beauty of the organization, is independent of the nature of the elements ordered.

Most of what we think of as visual forms are relations of colors worked into shapes, or relations of shapes worked into patterns; the form draws its ingredients from sensation and, at a higher level, combines simpler component forms into more complex and inclusive ones. But colors and shapes have no monopoly on form, nor do they possess any qualities which give the forms constructed of them a unique or an inevitable æsthetic status. A hundred insignificant plastic forms are created for every significant one, and the exceptional one owes its beauty not to the fact that it is plastic, but to the fact that it presents a rich and varied network of relations. If significant relations can likewise be established between elements of subject-matter, then the resulting "form" will be likewise beautiful. And that significant and beautiful relations *can* be established between such elements is the next conclusion to which our study leads. Inevitably linked with, yet distinct from, plastic form, there is possible a "subject-matter form"

—a network of organized relations established between the meanings or expressive elements evoked by ultra-plastic subject-matter.

I find myself embarrassed at this point by one of those difficulties of vocabulary which are so frequent in critical discussions of the arts. There is, to my knowledge, no satisfactory term denoting the particular realm of effect about which I now have to speak. Mr. Fry, following M. Mauron, has described it as "psychological" form, but this term seems to me an inadequate one. If thought of as applying to the psychological elements represented in the subject-matter, such as the traits that go to make up a character, then it seems too narrow to cover all the phases of subject-matter with which we must deal. The relation of a given architectural background, let us say, to a given type of action could hardly be envisaged under this connotation of the word. If, on the other hand, it is the psychology of the *observer* to which the term refers, then *all* the elements of æsthetic experience, plastic included, are psychological in nature.

In my own earlier studies of the question, I have used the term "representational" in this connection. But in the light of our present findings this is not adequate either. Plastic elements, as well as their ultra-plastic counterparts, are often representational; hence the two cannot properly be distinguished from each other by the use of this term. Furthermore, we shall need the latter to describe the combined plastic and ultra-plastic relations which constitute the form of a work of representational art as a whole, and which may thus appropriately be termed "representational" form.

After considerable labor and in the absence of any happier solution of the problem, I have decided to call ultra-plastic elements "associative" elements and the relations to which they give rise "associative" form. The term is suggested by the fact that ultra-plastic effects arise through the associative process and that, in visual art, they exist in association with plastic accompaniments. It provides a sufficient basis of distinction between plastic and ultra-plastic qualities and is sufficiently inclusive to indicate all the effects which we shall need to denote by it. At the same time, it leaves the more inclusive word "representational" for the further use just indicated.

If the suggested terminology be accepted, we have, then, three orders of form in representational art: plastic form, ultra-plastic or "associative" form, and the combination of these two in an embracing "representational" form.

Chapter VI

ASSOCIATIVE FORM

Let us begin our analysis of associative form by considering an example of character construction: the Rembrandt "Portrait of an Old Woman," Fig. 9. Plastic elements concurring in their expressive suggestions define a human figure; traits of that figure which we have learned to associate with certain life-qualities become expressive of personality or character.

Of what does the effect of character thus produced upon us by the picture consist? It is a combination, figuratively we might say a "pattern," of associated meanings. Sex is one. We read the character as that of a woman. Femininity becomes an element of the construction, here played but softly, most of its reverberations stilled by other and more dominant elements. Age is another. We see this person as an old person, whose time-worn face expresses the vicissitudes of life that lie behind and within. Growing out of this comes a third element, mellowness of character, the ripening and softening effect of the years. Related to this—slightly in contrast to it—a suggestion of sadness.

Other, less pronounced elements doubtless enter this character-form as well, but these are enough for our purpose. They indicate the fact that the "character" is a construction built up of relations between expressions of womanhood, old age, mellowness, spiritual resignation, and sadness. These expressions are combined in a certain individual measure—intangible *proportions*. They are blended with a particular degree of similarity or dissimilarity—intangible *unity* and *harmony,* little relieved in this case by the equally possible *contrast*. They are scaled in a selected order of importance, with old age dominant—intangible *emphasis*. They bear with certain weights of attraction upon our consciousness—intangible *balance*. Thus out of their combination an intangible *form* emerges. To use Charles Mauron's expressive metaphor, Rembrandt has "modelled" a "psychological volume." To express the same fact more literally, he has worked out a group of relations between associative elements, a group which is sufficiently absorbing in the play of mind which it stimulates, and sufficiently varied in what we might call its expressive "dimensions," to afford us an æsthetic experience equivalent to that aroused by a plastic form of intermediate intricacy. Less clearly defined than plastic form, the character-form on the other hand is freer and subtler, prolonging its vibrations further among elements to which conscious perception cannot penetrate; fading away into infinity like distance or the last notes of some hushed and solemn music.

It is true that an undeveloped observer may respond to the expressive elements involved in the character without going on to grasp the relations between them which organize them into form, just as the same observer will probably enjoy the sensuous appeal of colors without perceiving the formal significance of various color combinations and arrangements. One who sees the character in this manner will feel only its expressiveness and will be oblivious to its beauty of form. But to whatever degree an observer becomes conscious of the interrelation of the different traits within the character, in whatever measure he feels the relative unity and "profundity" of the characterization—and in a responsive observer, this must be to no inconsiderable extent—he is enjoying a purely formal beauty.

Fig. 10. Rembrandt. The Painter's Mother

Private Collection. (After Valentiner, *Rembrandt; Wiedergefundene Gemälde*)

Fig. 9. Rembrandt. Portrait of an Old Woman

Hermitage. (Bruckmann)

How much these intangible forms vary in their æsthetic significance, and how truly the representation of a character is a form, we become increasingly aware if we analyze a number of different character studies. Another Rembrandt (Fig. 10) will afford us an illuminating basis for comparison. The expressive elements which merge to create the character, the "materials" provided for the construction, are in part the same. The sex is again feminine, the age advanced. But instead of mellowness, spiritual resignation, and sadness, we have a suggestion of alertness with perhaps, in some elusive quizzical turn, the barest admixture of dry humor.

With one exception immediately to be noted, these associative elements, taken individually, are as significant as the corresponding elements of the former character, but the character as a whole will probably not impress most observers as nearly so significant. What accounts for the difference? Partly a deficiency in expression with regard to sex. We are hardly able to say from an examination of the figure itself whether the character is masculine or feminine. Our associative mechanism wavers between two possible connections and we find ourselves somewhat disturbed, like the lizards whom the biologists befuddle when they paint the representatives of one sex to look like those of the other. One of the elements to enter our character-form is thus an uncertain and, for that reason, unsatisfactory one.

But what concerns us even more directly is that the others, though satisfactory in themselves, hardly relate to each other in a significant manner. Old age, instead of finding successive harmonies in mellowness, resignation, and sadness, meets a contradiction in alertness and the stray touch of humor. Not that such characteristics are always incompatible with age, but that the precise expressions of the several traits here evoked hardly seem compatible with each other. The inter-relation of elements, instead of being clear and finely organized, is to some degree discordant; the resulting form to that extent disjointed. As we are accustomed to say of literary characters subject to similar defects, this character "lacks unity."

Another defect of character construction which we frequently encounter in visual art is superficiality or "shallowness." Examples are not wanting in the works of Fra Angelico, Perugino, Raphael, and the earlier Correggio. The women at the left of Raphael's "Marriage of the Virgin" afford striking instances, particularly those at the two ends of the group. Unquestionably unified, they fall short in the opposite direction. They lack sufficient variety or complexity. .They involve only two elements: they are obviously feminine, as obviously at that period of life between youth and maturity. Search as I will I find no other traits. Sweetness, earnestness, intelligence, vivacity, coyness, a score of other qualities that might combine with femininity and youth to enrich these characters, are absent from them. Two elements are not enough to create rich relations. Consequently these characters remain blank and shallow, hardly more than lifeless human masks. They are, as we say, "mere types" lacking in depth and individuality.

What we ordinarily speak of as the "expression" of a face or character in a work of art thus proves in reality to be a compound of many different "expressions," using the term now in its limited sense to signify meanings expressively evoked. The great creators of character —Rembrandt, Velasquez, Daumier, Toulouse-Lautrec—are those who are able to conjure up the distinctive separate essences of many and varied traits, and who are further able—a still more difficult task—to blend these essences with each other in richly organized relations:

unified, multiple in their harmonies, and finely scaled in their emphasis. Such a result can be achieved only by the application, within the intangible realm of expression, of a power of selection, purification, emphasis upon essentials, and significant organization, similar to that exercised by the gifted artist in dealing with plastic elements.

Too elusive to permit of more than approximate analysis in the case of individual character construction, the workings of form in representation are easier to follow when we turn to more inclusive networks of associative relations. One such network may be woven of the relations between one character and another, when several appear in the same work. A simple yet finely organized example may be seen in Titian's "Madonna of the Cherries" (Fig. 11).

Religious dignity and aristocratic distinction run through all the characters as pervading sources of harmony—associative equivalents of the ambient "Venetian glow." Within them appear the contrasts of man with woman, of comparative old age with maturity and with childhood—equivalents of those broad chords of blue and red and green which plastically appear within the golden ambience. And through this harmony and these contrasts, further and now very subtly interrelating the characters and distinguishing between them in their order of relative importance, runs a scale of emphasis in which the greatest force of attraction is given to the Child, a shade less to the Madonna, with succeeding degrees of subordination upon the remaining figures. Thus harmony, contrast, and emphasis, merged in a governing unity, bind the characters together into a design of no small beauty. How much the effect would suffer were any of these relations disturbed! Were a Frans Hals witch or a Toulouse-Lautrec bar-maid to replace the Madonna, into what jangling discord would the harmony give way! Were the characters all men or all women, how much the variety of the design would be diminished! Were even these same characters presented in a manner which gave them all equal prominence, how far the relations would slip from their present subtle diversity toward uniform and monotonous repetition!

In his "Presentation of the Virgin," Titian extends such interrelations between characters to a scale approaching grandeur. A group of characters akin to, though considerably larger than, that just considered—the Virgin's suite—becomes as a whole the component of a larger form, a grouping of groups, in which this first aristocratic group is echoed by a second, that of the priests and their attendant choir boys, and both these groups receive a contrast in characters from other walks of life: beggars, a peasant woman selling eggs, onlookers some of whom offset the prevalent seriousness with an approach to humor and the grotesque. The range in dignity between the dominant characters and some of those who serve as foils is hardly less far-reaching than that which divides the saints from the gargoyles on a Gothic cathedral, and hardly less magnificent in the force of contrast derived from its bold juxtaposition of opposites. Given the relative "volume" of each individual character, the relations within each group and the relations between groups, the formal beauty of such a character composition is probably as great as that attained by most of the single plastic elements, say line or mass, even in the hands of great painters.

Other works which come to mind as important examples of character composition include Gozzoli's frescoes, particularly those in the Pisan Campo Santo, Veronese's feast scenes, and Rubens's mythological inventions; also various paintings, and even more strikingly "Christ Healing the Sick" and numerous other etchings, by Rembrandt. To

Fig. 11. Titian. Madonna of the Cherries
Imperial Gallery, Vienna. (Bruckmann)

these might be added certain of the portrait groups by Velasquez, Hals, and Goya. Nor have more recent painters abandoned the resources of character composition. One recalls instances delicious in their subtlety, even if rarely extensive in their range, among the works of Daumier, Manet, Degas, and Toulouse-Lautrec. To cite but three details from these many possible examples, old as well as new, what contrast could be more effective than that which Rembrandt brings into the "Night Watch" by introducing one small maiden in the midst of so much animated soldiery? Or more exquisite than that which Goya establishes by placing the bird-shy little prince between the arrogant queen and the pompous king in his "Family of Charles IV"? Or more startling than that which Manet creates, in his "Balcony," by opposing the moronic vacuity of the maid to the piercing and almost diabolical intelligence of the mistress?

The principle thus illustrated in respect to character, whereby the relations of expressive elements within and between characters are seen to constitute potential aspects of form, can be applied with equal force to the other associative "means"—to "action," to "setting," and to the more elusive effects of "mood" and of "imaginative appeal." Each is a compound of meanings derived in the first instance from our associations with various types of objects or events. Each compound consists of a series of intermingled associations which, as associations, may exert an *expressive* appeal but which, co-existing in relationship to each other, involve an organization or a *form*. Examples of each of these additional sources of effect could be analyzed, as we have analyzed examples of character, and would be found to involve their relative amplitudes and unities, their relative degrees of harmony and contrast and emphasis; in a word, their potential beauty of form. Since we are concerned in the present volume, however, only with the general principles underlying the relation of representation to form, and not with a description of the various specific effects to which representation may give rise, and since the analysis of these additional associative means, studied individually, would in no way modify the principles already considered, we must leave them for treatment elsewhere and pass on to the next step in our main development.

This step consists in recognizing that the several associative means, themselves already networks of relations between expressive elements, in turn give rise to more inclusive combinations. Character, action, and setting are commonly brought together in the same work, interacting upon each other in the larger sphere thus created. A given action seems appropriate to (in unity and harmony with) a given character; a given setting reinforces, or it may be conflicts with or neutralizes, the effect of a given action. The component networks of relations within each separate means merge with each other, like waters tributary to a growing stream, setting up more complex and more extensive relations which eventually absorb all the expressed meanings of the picture and so constitute its total associative form.

These more extensive relationships have been involved to some degree even in the simpler works which have served as our illustrations of the relations within and between characters. Our Rembrandt "Old Woman" (Fig. 9) is not exclusively a character construction. Action is reduced to a minimum, but is nevertheless present in the quietly seated posture, the folded hands, the gaze of inward absorption. No other action could harmonize so well with the central motif which the character establishes. Setting, in the costume, chair, and background, plays a larger rôle in the total effect and plays that rôle in perfect keeping with the context of which it is to form a part. Rembrandt has not chosen for this work one of those richly jewelled costumes with plumed hats or floral wreaths which he loved to invent and which he used to such rich effect in many of his figure studies. Appropriate to the lyric appeal of Saskia's young womanhood, these would be as out of season here as mayflowers at that autumn hour

> "when leaves like corpses fall,
> And saps all retrocede."

Restraint, sobriety, indifference to worldly show, are the notes that must now be sounded, and Rembrandt sounds them softly and beautifully in the simplicity of the costume, the subordination of the chair, the plainness of a background free of all accessories.

Thus action and setting merge into a unity with character, extending and enriching the harmony of meanings which the character began, and at the same time affording that character dominance through their own finely felt degrees of subordination. Within the whole range of meanings which the picture involves, no single one, not the slightest associative reverberation, but takes its appointed place in the fabric of expressive relations. The total associative form is flawless in its unity, many-echoed in its harmony, profound in the unfathomable intricacy of its multiple and elusive interrelations. The same can hardly be said of our second Rembrandt portrait, in which neither action nor setting achieves relationship with the character to at all the same degree of significance.

Similar considerations hold true of the Titian "Madonna of the Cherries" (Fig. 11). Again the harmony is perfect and, so far as concerns the mood of dignity, it is in a similar key. But in other respects, the governing motif being different, different notes are required to harmonize with it. Action, though still restrained within bounds compatible with religious feeling, becomes somewhat more pronounced in order to avoid any suggestion of lifelessness or stiffness. Setting receives greater elaboration in order to strike a note of restrained splendor, a note appropriate to characters who inhabit a world lacking neither in material riches nor in spiritual sensitivity to their appropriate use.

How varied the relation between setting and characters may be in pictures of this type and how easily that relation may be disturbed, is made evident by comparison with other examples. In Veronese's "Marriage of St. Catherine," the setting occupies a much larger area of the picture and is at the same time made emphatic through the introduction of elaborate cloud effects, festooned columns, a carved dais, and richly patterned textiles. These properties compete with, if they do not surpass, the character and action in relative force of attraction. As a result, one may be led to question whether the associative form does not suffer from a lack of satisfactory emphasis.

When Tintoretto, striking the contrast between a supernatural action and a proletarian setting, stages his San Rocco "Annunciation" in a peasant kitchen, with a decrepit chair, a dilapidated wall, and other commonplace accessories in evidence, he presses his associative relations to the limits of a *tour de force*. But when Rembrandt sets his religious episodes in similar surroundings of homely low life, he finds an entirely new relation between his associative elements. The splendor and elevation of the Italian form are gone, but they are replaced by an expressiveness of love for faltering humanity, of spiritual values immanent in common things; an effect achieved with an internal coherence no less complete than the other and one equally possible as a development of the germinating religious theme.

As a final example of inclusive associative relations, let us consider a work from that large class in which action rather than character provides the main motif. In this case, we have a reordering of the three chief associative means within the form, action becoming dominant and receiving support from character and setting. We shall take as an example El Greco's "Agony in the Garden" (Fig. 12).

The major action, that of Christ receiving the cup from the angel, is interwoven with two closely related "sub-plots," at the left that of the sleeping disciples, at the right that of the soldiers approaching to take Christ captive. How beautifully these three strands complete each other in the action-form! The major theme of suffering and supplication is intensified by the apparition of the soldiers, through whose offices fate hastens to its tragic end; intensified anew by the frailty of the disciples who, unable to overcome their weakness, leave their leader to support his trial in isolation, unbefriended by human support.

The interrelation of these three themes was, of course, already significant in the literary sources by which the picture was inspired and can hardly be credited to El Greco's invention. Not so the remaining elements of the associative form. The visualization of each of these actions in itself, the degree of emphasis which each was to receive pictorially, together with the other effects to which we shall shortly refer, all presented themselves to the artist as creative pictorial problems, problems toward the solution of which literary sources could offer little aid. How fully, in the position and gesture of the main figure, he has "modelled" the dramatic "volume" of the dominant theme with its intermixture of contrasting and conflicting meanings—suffering and determination, supplication and acceptance, desire to escape and will to remain.

Compare this figure with the equivalent one in Perugino's version of the same subject, Fig. 13. Christ kneels as before, but in a stable posture and with a meditative calm, as though absorbed by tranquil inward vision. Note also how the foreground position of the disciples gives this secondary theme an emphasis equal to that of the main one, while at the same time the greater emphasis on character in the disciples and their proximity to Christ seem to provide him with a degree of human fellowship in his trial and thus lessen the dramatic intensity which both the biblical and the El Greco versions achieve. Only in one respect can the Perugino treatment of the action be granted a degree of success. The approaching soldiers, by their number, their active movements, and the way in which they seem to be closing in from all sides, achieve with considerable force the desired effect of impending doom. In this respect, the small and orderly band of the El Greco version is perhaps less effective. Taken as a whole, however, the El Greco compounds its many action elements into a pattern forceful in its unity, rich in its harmonies and contrasts, and clearly ordered in its emphasis; a pattern which elaborates to the point of profound significance the central motive of spiritual suffering in the face of an oncoming tragic fate.

Let us now consider the relations which El Greco establishes between this central motif of his subject-matter as expressed in the action and the character and setting by which that action is accompanied. Character receives little more development than is essential as a foundation for the action. It becomes an independent source of effect only in the

Fig. 12. El Greco.
Agony in the Garden
Arthur Sachs Collection, Paris

Fig. 13. Perugino.
Agony in the Garden
Uffizi. (Alinari)

Christ and there, apart from the inevitable traits of manhood and maturity, finds its chief extension in spiritual earnestness. The emphasis on this trait provides the necessary point of affinity between character and action, enabling the characterization to reinforce the action by making clear its relevance to the personality of the principal actor. The strong degree of subordination imposed upon the secondary actions reduces the other actors to a scale at which psychological individuality is not discernible, making of them, as it were, supernumeraries. The resulting emphasis upon the character of Christ is effective as an ordering of the character-form and, as we have already seen, supports the action by increasing the effect of isolation and loneliness in the central figure.

Perugino's version lacks both these significant inter-character relationships, and further suffers from the fact that spirituality receives no greater emphasis in the characterization of Christ than in any of the disciples. Indeed, the faces of the two younger disciples tend to produce a more spiritual effect than that of the Christ himself, so that competition between characters enters in a respect in which we feel that the dominant character should be outstanding.

But it is from setting that El Greco draws his richest harmonies with the governing motif set by the action. What world will echo best, through qualities associated with inanimate things, the quality of the human experience here represented for us? That is the question to which the artist must paint an answer and he can paint it successfully only if guided by sensitivity to subtle affinities between the intangible elements of expression. El Greco's answer is conclusive.

One rock occupies the right foreground, another and larger one forms the immediate background to the figure of Christ. What objects could be more akin to his experience? They are hard, comfortless, repellent; so is the way before him. But they are firm, unyielding, immovable; so is he. The upright rock leans slightly, as though its stability were not absolute, while yet it is; so Christ beseeches that the cup may pass, yet remains ready to drink it. Behind we see congealed clouds, openings of starless sky, the pale indifference of a half-shrouded moon. Rocks, clouds, darkness, and filtered moonlight—such are the essential elements of this setting. Each is an echo of the moment of life that is transpiring; each sounds with that moment in somber, minor harmonies. Again we have an associative form in which contributions from action, character, and setting are combined in a single unified network of relations; a form as profound in the complexity of its elements as it is unified in the organization to which they are brought.

In respect to setting, a comparison with the Perugino version is again illuminating. Instead of overhanging rock, we have a pleasant landscape for a background; instead of night and clouds, daylight and a fair sky. A distant city invites our thoughts away from what should be the inescapable tension of the action. The scene is thus inviting rather than oppressive; if not discordant with the action, at least indifferent to its spirit. Action and setting neutralize each other and we can abandon ourselves neither to the lyric charm of the one nor to the tragic tension of the other. Above all we do not experience that cumulative effect of heightened intensity which results in the El Greco from the reinforcement of each successive wave of meaning by others which follow in the same direction.

El Greco, we say, surpasses Perugino in his sense for the dramatic. In the terms of our present study, this "sense for the dramatic" reduces itself to a mastery of certain aspects of form—a sensitivity to relations which enables the artist to amplify a dramatic motif into a richly organized and compelling form in which all the possibilities of that motif are developed and expanded for the achievement of a maximum total effect. And we may note in passing that the associative form thus created is as uniquely El Greco's, both in personal quality and in subtlety of organization, as is the accompanying plastic form from which it emanates.

Were further instances of the relation of one associative means to another desirable, they would flood to hand. Tura in his "St. Jerome," Mantegna in his "Crucifixion," Titian in his "Entombment"—not to extend the list further—had preceded El Greco in harmonizing austere or mournful settings with similar phases of experience. But when Mantegna sets the muses of Parnassus dancing among rocks, austerity of setting being with him a convention rather than an effect selected for its appropriateness to given combinations, the harmony gives way to discord. Severity is here out of place with the lyric effect started by character, action, and costume. As in our Perugino, the associative relations are broken and the form is dissatisfying in consequence.

Fra Angelico finds happier echoes for a lyric motif when he places the "elect" of his Paradise in fields deep with grass and sweet with flowers; so does Giorgione in the harmonies between caressing landscapes and the human form which characterize his "Sleeping Venus" and his "Pastoral Concert"; so also does Veronese in the luxuriant silks and dreamy skies which accompany the love theme of his "Mars and Venus," and in the monumental architecture, splendid robes, and princely table accessories which quicken the mood of his feast scenes. Or, if we turn to themes requiring more sedate accompaniment, we can find examples of the same logic of organization underlying an entirely different range of effects. We feel at once, for instance, the harmony between the spiritual theme of Angelico's "Annunciation" and the cloistral architecture which forms its setting; between the similar theme of Rembrandt's smaller "Emmaus" and the noble dignity of the interior in which the artist has enclosed it. But we are far from feeling such a harmony in Crivelli's version of the "Annunciation," where architecture of palatial stamp, an exuberant display of worldly riches, and an ungoverned wealth of secondary episode, crowd out the unobtrusive major, or nominally major, motif.

To summarize the results obtained from the study of our fourth stratum, ultra-plastic representation is not limited to an expressive function—to the appeal which subject-matter has, merely as subject-matter, because of its associations with our experience in life. The representation of any given subject is a fabric of relations between numberless individual associations—the intangible "elements" of the realm of expression. The relations between these elements are capable of organization and when organized constitute form. When carried to a point of high development by great pictorial composers, the associative form thus created becomes "significant form" indeed, delighting the perceptive mind with elusive yet compelling relations, with infinitely varied harmonies and contrasts, with beautifully modelled "psychological volumes." Thus even in its ultra-plastic aspects, subject-matter reveals a capacity for the enrichment of formal beauty.

If this be accepted, we must revise two conceptions which have had considerable influence in modern criticism. One is the assumption that visual form is uniquely a plastic phenomenon; or to state the same idea differently, that only plastic elements lend themselves effectively to the creation of form, and that, in consequence, representational elements lie outside the pale of consideration for those who are capable of discerning formal beauty. In point of fact, plastic and representational elements occupy, in this respect, precisely analogous positions. Neither group gives rise to form unless brought together in significant relationships; when thus brought together, both groups give rise to form. Form is in no sense necessarily or uniquely plastic, and plastic elements have no monopoly over the resources of formal beauty.

The second conception to be modified is that, still widely current, which distinguishes between form and subject-matter, or form and "content," as separable and more or less competing sources of effect, either of which may be valued independently of the other. From the æsthetic point of view, the modern critic who excludes subject-matter from the sphere of consideration holds a position similar to that of the novice who sees beauty *only* in subject-matter, and also that of the archæologist or art historian who values art chiefly for its historical "content"—for what it represents of religious or social ideas; for what it embodies of the life of the period that produced it. Observers of all these types make a distinction where, æsthetically, no distinction exists. The critic who disdains subject-matter misses part of the *form* of the work he is studying; he is blind to one phase of its potential æsthetic value. The novice enjoys the expressive appeal which the critic disdains and enjoys little else, missing the form and its æsthetic significance almost entirely, but unconsciously supporting the critic's contention that there is nothing in subject-matter *but* an expressive appeal. The archæologist and historian who place "content" above form have hardly entered the æsthetic sphere at all. They are studying art to be sure, but they are not studying æsthetic values. They are considering art in its extraneous relations to life, as a phase of history and sociology.

Æsthetically, subject-matter, the representation of things or presentation of ideas, can no more be called the content of form than flesh can be called the content of a living body. Without the one, the other cannot exist. There is no such thing as form without content (the charge of the novice and historian against abstract art) or content without form (the charge of the abstractionist against an interest in subject-matter). There is only material formed or formless. If the material is formed, it ceases, æsthetically, to have any independent existence as material. It is absorbed into the form and becomes part of it, as assimilated food becomes part of the body. If the material is formless then, apart from any sensuous or expressive appeal which it may have, it is æsthetically insignificant; which is to say that the work of art embodying it is a poor one. To study the "content" in any respect except its relation to, and degree of assimilation into, the form is to study non-æsthetic elements. In this respect it will be observed that we reach, by means of critical analysis, a conclusion at which Croce had long since arrived from the opposite direction through philosophical deduction.

CHAPTER VII

ARE ASSOCIATIVE EFFECTS LEGITIMATE?

Before proceeding to our study of the final extension of visual form, which results from the interrelationships between associative effects and their plastic accompaniments, it may be well to pause for a moment to consider certain questions concerning the associative elements themselves. Since the advent of the abstractionist point of view, they have been under suspicion. Charges have been advanced against them which, if true, would exclude them from a legitimate place in visual art. We must now examine these charges.

It may be said, in the first place, that plastic and associative effects cannot be observed simultaneously; that to focus attention upon the one is to remove it from the other, hence that associative effects distract attention from plastic ones and disturb the unity of visual form.

While the two are never entirely severed from each other in our consciousness, we must admit that both cannot be dominant there at the same time. To whatever extent we concentrate attention upon the one, sharpening it into a foreground of perception, we remove the focus of attention from the other, reducing it to a diffused background of perception. This follows automatically from the fact, generally recognized in psychology, that the mind works on a focussing principle. It cannot concentrate its full powers of observation upon more than one facet of experience at a time.

There is no reason, however, why this fact should militate against the development of associative effects in visual art. It applies with equal force among the plastic elements themselves. If we study the color of a painting at all attentively, observing its relative freshness and structural quality, the choice of individual colors which it involves and the degree to which they have been combined to achieve harmony, balance, and other aspects of design, then during the course of these observations, we necessarily become more or less oblivious to line, space, and the other plastic elements with which these color effects are interwoven. Creative practice sometimes perpetuates similar concentrations in art. In proportion as the Impressionists focussed their attention on color and light, their pictures became effects of color and light: mass, space, linear design and other potential plastic qualities faded out of them.

But it does not follow because we cannot concentrate attention fully upon all the aspects of a rich plastic creation at the same moment, that a work limited to a few plastic elements is better than one with many. A uniformly colored disk would then be preferable to a decorative pattern; a pattern to the intricate orchestration of all the plastic elements in a great painting. Rather we prize most highly the work which involves an inexhaustible number of elements; which satisfies our separate explorations of color and line and many other sources of effect— provided always that its effects include significant relations between the several elements and so culminate in a governing unity.

As already implied, there is never any real severance between the elements momentarily in the focus of attention and those beyond it. The latter always remain as a background of perception, fading away from the former and providing a transitional zone through which the attention is drawn to successive aspects of the total combination of elements. Our experience, like the objective combination of elements itself, is a *continuum,* but it is a continuum of changing aspects unfolded by the activity of a constantly shifting mental focus.

Whether that experience would be of a higher order if we were capable of grasping a complex whole as a total unchanging unity would be a bootless question to raise, since we are not so constituted as to make this possible. But the experience permitted by our actual constitution has this to be said in its favor: the shifting of attention from one aspect of the work to another is a source of repeated renewals of interest and enjoyment, an exercise of exploration and discovery which prolongs our experience and at the same time, as we rise to the perception of more inclusive relations and finally to the total-relation pervading the whole work, affords us a cumulative increase in the intensity of that experience and so may lead eventually to those ultimate perceptions and ultimate responses which mark the summits of æsthetic experience.

Associative effects form no exception to the principle just considered. When the mental focus shifts to them, other qualities blur off accordingly. But this fact in no way limits their significance or their appropriateness to visual art. Provided they ultimately unify with their plastic accompaniments—a matter which we still have to examine— they too may take appointed places both in the objective combination of elements and in the continuum of experience through which we perceive it. Their presence is merely an indication that the work possesses additional facets of significance, hence that the total experience which it embodies and conveys is a richer and more complex one than it would be if they were not there. The basic second-stratum plastic

elements, without losing any of their second-stratum plastic significance, have been employed to create other spheres of effect; first the
third-stratum plastic qualities and now the fourth-stratum associative
qualities, expanding our experience from sphere to sphere, like circles
widening where a stone has been dropped in water. To expand as far
as possible, to comprehend the maximum range of being, and so to
move us with cumulative force as we are swept from sphere to sphere
—such would seem to be the aim of art in its ultimate manifestations.
This aim associative effects help visual art to accomplish. Without
them it would be restricted at limits only a few steps beyond abstraction; limits which we have seen to be far from including all the
possibilities of art.

Nor, I believe, is the function of associative elements in visual art
purely one of enrichment. On the principle of renewal through change
which was mentioned above, the very removal of attention from plastic
effects which has been held against associative ones may be a means
of prolonging and "balancing" our æsthetic experience. Judging by the
feel of my own perceptive mechanism as I grasp it through introspec-
tion, I suspect strongly that it works on some alternating principle
which makes the possibility of passing from one sphere of effect to another very propitious to its functioning. We know that a single color,
contemplated exclusively for any length of time, fatigues the eye.
Visual comfort demands a varied combination of colors, presumably
because such a combination gives balanced play to the various sets of
retinal "cones." Earlier in the present study we noted that a sense of
mental stress results from the prolonged and unbroken contemplation
of abstract plastic effects. It seems not unlikely that balanced functioning of the mind involves a recurrent alternation of the focus of atten-

tion between plastic and associative effects.[1] Such an alternation would provide the maximum diversity of experience possible within the continued contemplation of a total unity. Thus it would presumably afford maximum repose while at the same time permitting maximum economy of perceptive energy and maximum duration of perceptive enjoyment.

To study this question in greater detail would lead us away from art into psychology. Perhaps enough has been said, however, to indicate that an alternation of attention between plastic and associative effects is only a larger sweep of a process involved in all perception, that there appears to be no reason for ascribing a negative significance to it, and that in all probability it plays a positive part in refreshing and prolonging æsthetic experience.

A second objection to associative effects might be raised by saying that they depended upon the representation of *extra-visual* experience and that visual art should limit itself to purely visual elements. But as the earlier sections of the present study have shown, a large number of the plastic elements—all those lying outside our second-stratum—also depend upon the interpretation of visual data by recourse to non-visual experience. Were we to limit painting and sculpture to elements provided in complete form by vision, then color, line, shape, and size would be the only elements available to them. But in the more liberal sense of the term, the other plastic elements like mass and space are also visual; that is to say, indicated by visual elements when, through non-visual experience, we have learned how to interpret them.

In this larger sense, the ultra-plastic elements of representation are

[1] *Cf.* Vernon Lee, *The Beautiful,* pp. 106 *et seq.;* 119.

also visual. Though we must have had non-visual experience to be able to read them, they are an integral part of the significance of visual stimuli. They cannot be legitimately excluded unless we wish to limit ourselves to visual stimuli uninterpreted by *any* of their meanings, in which case we should have to restrict art to the sphere of geometrical pattern. That such a restriction could result only in loss, is evident. It is the task and the opportunity of the artist to exploit as fully as possible *all* the capacities of his medium; to make his elements a source of impressions as rich and complex as possible. The more numerous and subtle the reverberations he is able to produce from the physical properties of his medium, which in the first instance are all that he has to work with, the more impressive will be the resulting effect and, as I have tried to show in connection with representation, the richer and more varied will be the elements at his disposal for organization into form.

The third and most common objection against which associative effects have to defend themselves is the charge, current in recent decades, that they are "literary" rather than pictorial. In part this is a variation of the objection just considered—that they are extra-visual rather than visual. But stated in this more general form, the objection involves a larger field and calls for further examination.

If the usage of the term "literary" which we here encounter were recognized as purely descriptive, it might be admitted. It would then mean "resembling literature in certain respects" or "having certain effects in common with literature." We have already recognized that ultra-plastic representation occurs in the stratum of associated meanings. A similar stratum occurs in literature, indeed, holds the dominant place there. Hence literature has come to be accepted as the type *par excellence* of representational art and conversely all ultra-plastic representation is associated in the mind with literature. To use the term "literary" in the resulting comparative sense is merely to say, in figurative language, that both pictorial and literary art are representational and that, since ultra-plastic representation reaches its greatest extension and achieves its greatest dominance in literature, all such representation can be conveniently described in terms of its most developed type as "literary."

But when the meaning of the term "literary," as applied to visual art, is extended to mean "copied from and proper only to literature; out of place in visual art," then we must examine our grounds closely before we accept it. It would seem to arise from an assumption that each of the arts, or at least each related group of arts, occupies a territory exclusively its own; an assumption that if a given type of effect is proper to the arts of one group or medium, it is for that reason improper to those of any other.

A moment's reflection should suffice to convince one that such an assumption is unfounded. Each art possesses certain resources which are uniquely its own and in each the total effect, the relative place given to the various component elements, will be equally distinctive. But at the same time, each art overlaps others, possessing resources in common with those others which are proper to them all. There is a "musical" element in literature and to a less extent in visual art. There is a "pictorial" element in literature. There may be "architectural" elements in music. The common use made of these terms implies no disparagement; in fact, when we describe Bach's fugues as "architectural" or Renoir's color as "symphonic" in its surge and harmony, we use these terms in praise and not in blame. We are simply describing an effect, common to two arts, in terms of that which carries it farthest.

So when we describe associative effects in visual art as "literary," we need imply no blame and indeed, so far as concerns the presence and use of those effects, there seems no legitimate reason for attaching blame. Such effects are not, in any sense, transpositions from literature into painting or sculpture of material which only writers can discern and express at first hand. They could and would exist in visual art irrespective of the fact that literature happens to create partially similar effects. They are inspired directly by a visual response to the world we live in; by what the eye can see and the mind learns to associate with its seeing. They are, in short, immediately apprehensible in visual experience, interpreted through the expressiveness which that experience spontaneously and inevitably acquires.

It is true that the pictorial versions of religious and mythological themes have often taken their point of departure from data given in literary sources. This circumstance may influence us in according priority to literature in the creation of representational effects, but it is purely a historical, and not an æsthetic, circumstance. It could have been, and in many cases has been, quite otherwise. The Assyrians did not wait for historical records to inspire the portrayal of their wars and hunting scenes, nor did Daumier need literary models to show him the pictorial possibilities, associative as well as plastic, of a wrangle between jurors. As much representational art has been inspired directly from nature as from literary sources or, if by chance the proportion is at present in favor of the latter, that circumstance is changing rapidly under social conditions which make art less a handmaid of religion and more a quest for distinctive values of its own.

Even in the case of earlier work which was inspired by literary sources, or by religious traditions which had first been given literary embodiment, the material provided for the pictorial versions was usually slight. Had the literary sources been in any adequate sense pictorial, there would have been little call for actual pictures, still less would there have been any creative problem which could inspire the efforts of a Giotto, a Titian, or an El Greco. At best the text affords certain elementary data as to the types of character or action in terms of which the work is to be conceived. The visualization of the characters, the pictorial rendering of the action, above all the amplitude of visual realization and visual form-building, are matters in which the artist has to depend upon his own creative powers and for help with which he must turn to a direct observation of the world about him. And they are matters of no small complexity. If the visual rendering of biblical themes had been a mere exercise in transcription, Leonardo need not have vexed the prior of Santa Maria delle Gracie by "wasting" so much time in thought before the wall prepared to receive his "Last Supper," nor would there be an appreciable difference between Leonardo's "Last Supper" and that of any other interpreter.

It is significant to note in the present connection that conversely to the assumption which we have been opposing, many of our supposed literary conceptions have been strongly influenced by visual art. If, when we read the Gospels, we have in our minds a visual image of the appearance of Jesus, that is not because the Gospels themselves provide us with any such image or because any clue to his appearance is obtainable from either literary or historical sources except for the one fact, probably suppressed from our visualization, that Jesus was a Jew. If we have such an image, it is only because sculptors and glass-makers and painters, drawing their inspiration from an ideal and their materials from the observation of human types around them, have achieved a visual characterization sufficiently convincing to be accepted by large numbers of people as a reality and carried back into their interpretation of the written records.

To say that El Greco should not have visualized the scene on Geth-semane because it had been narrated in the Gospels would be equiva-lent to saying that Claude Lorraine should not have painted scenes of classical grandeur because that grandeur had been given previous literary embodiment by Homer, or that Degas and Renoir should not have pictured the life of nineteenth-century France because it had already been described by Flaubert and Zola. Meanings arise in life, not in art. The artist discovers them in his contemplation of the world about him. He discovers further that the intrinsic qualities of various media lend themselves to the expression of these meanings in varying degrees. To whatever degree that may be in any given art, these meanings are a phase of the artist's natural material. He will spontane-ously take advantage of the expressiveness which they confer upon his medium and will pursue it to whatever limits that medium permits. In arts like sculpture and painting which represent natural beings and things—the same which literature itself represents—these beings and things will inevitably bring meanings with them and to that extent the visual arts are necessarily and properly "literary." As we have seen this is no more than a picturesque way of stating the obvious fact that they are representational.

Indeed we may go further. We have seen that representation is inevitable in visual art for plastic reasons if for no other. With equal inevitability, it brings associative meanings with it. The artist may be free to decide how far he wishes to cultivate such meanings, but as to the presence of some minimum of them in his work he has little choice. And since they are there in any case, since they exist as elements which must bear some relation, either positive or negative, to each other and to their plastic accompaniments, the fundamental question from the æsthetic point of view is how far they have been organized. If they remain external to the formal significance of the work, then they can be only so much impurity in the total form, so much *impedimenta* which it must strain itself to carry. In other words, associative elements are usually present whether we like it or not, and will play a negative part in the work of art if the artist does not see to it that they are made to play a positive one.

They do play a negative part in a considerable number of important works, including some which are plastically of high value. We have noted elsewhere that Angelico, Raphael, and Correggio are frequently shallow in their characterization. Titian himself often suffers from a similar defect in his characterization of women, which rarely attains a "psychological volume" comparable to that of his profoundly "modelled" men.

Tintoretto sometimes falls short in his treatment of action, allowing the exaggerated movement which he loved for its rhythmical and dramatic effects, and with which he often obtained such superb results, to become a mannerism and to break the unity of the associative form. In such cases, the defect usually arises from the display made of dramatic movement in developing a non-dramatic theme. Associative relations are started in two conflicting keys, the physical and the psychological components of the action fail to integrate satisfactorily, and the movement stands apart from the associative fabric as an "accentuation." In its intrinsic beauty but lack of adequate integration, it presents an associative parallel to much of Botticelli's line.

Vermeer often fails to carry an organization which is significant in its plastic aspect over into an equally significant achievement of "human values." Human beings tend to sink to the level of still-life; in fact they are often less adequately represented than the objects of still-life around them, which casts a slight pallor over the work as though it were still-born. Velasquez in most of his religious pictures, magnificent though they are in plastic and in realistic associative values, creates a conflict between his realism and the visionary scenes which he ostensibly represents. Hence he fails to achieve the "religious elevation" of artists like Giotto and Titian or the "deep mysticism" of El Greco.

Manet in many of his Spanish pictures, such as "Mlle. Victorine in the Costume of an Espada" and "Toreador Saluting," invokes a world which he fails to establish, ostensibly painting scenes of dramatic reality but leaving us with an effect of models artificially posed in a studio. He has apparently been intrigued by a given realm of associations and has incorporated them in his work as expressive meanings, but has failed to develop them richly and subtly and to organize them into a convincing and seemingly inevitable fabric of relations. They remain "superficial" associative effects in a manner closely analogous to that in which color may be plastically superficial.

Finally, we need only remind ourselves of Doctor Barnes' estimate of Matisse to perceive again that no degree of plastic genius is adequate to the highest achievements of art if arrested at a "decorative" level; if, in other words, it fails to carry through to representational, hence in some measure to associative, as well as abstract significance. In short, associative effects, far from being "literary" in the sense of inappropriate to visual art, inevitably enter mature visual forms, affect the organization of those forms, and play a part which cannot be overlooked in determining their total value.

An attempt has sometimes been made to discriminate between the legitimate and the illegitimate use of subject-matter in visual art in terms of internal completeness in the visual representation. If, it is said, the desired associative effect can be conveyed directly by the painting or statue, without resort to external explanations in language and without necessitating special information on the part of the observer, then it is proper to the art involved. If not, its use is illegitimate, resulting in a kind of "program picture" which oversteps the bounds of visual art and pursues in one medium effects proper only to another. Thus Doctor Barnes writes: "In so far as the spectator . . . must depend upon the resources of his own knowledge to read the qualities of the subject-matter into the artistic representation, the effect is illegitimate. An artist, however, is entitled to such effects as he can really incorporate into his rendering of a subject."[2]

At first sight, the distinction appears simple and the principle based upon it useful as a standard of judgment. The supposedly "illegitimate" effects, or extensions of meaning into spheres requiring external explanation, would most commonly result (a) from attempts at factual identification of objects or characters and (b) from the representation of action which depended for its full significance upon our acquaintance with some sequence of events not shown in the picture.

[2] *The Art in Painting,* p. 49.

The distinction between internal and external meanings, in the case of factual identification, may be made clear by reference to the "Madonna of the Cherries" (Fig. 11). The work is intended to portray specific beings and indeed represents them in their specific individuality, but it gives us no clue to any significance which they may have beyond what is conveyed by their appearance. We behold men, children, and a woman; we perceive that they represent an elevated station in life; we recognize philosophical traits of mind in the men and in all the characters spiritual refinement. At some such level of acquaintance we must stop and there, so far as concerns the essence of pictorial contemplation, we are content to stop, for we have already been afforded a vision of interesting beings, significantly "modelled" and beautifully related to each other and to their world. Nevertheless it may be the wish of the artist, or of his patron, to press our acquaintance with the subject further: to inform us whence these beings come and who they are. Sooner or later, if we contemplate the picture long, we are likely to wonder as much ourselves. These questions the painter cannot answer by direct pictorial means. If he considers it necessary to inform us on these points, he must resort to ultra-pictorial expedients.

Titian has not scrupled to introduce one such expedient into the present work, though only as a minor detail and probably as much for compositional as for informative reasons. On the scroll held by the child at the right, we can decipher the word ". . . AGNUS"—lamb. Thus indirectly we are provided with a clue to the identity of one of the characters, presumably the other child. Raphael used the device openly in giving one of the figures in his "Parnassus" a scroll inscribed "SAPPHO" and Michelangelo similarly labelled the prophets and the sibyls of the Sistine vault. Many works by the primitives and certain portraits by Tintoretto, Dürer, and Velasquez come to mind as further examples of the use of inscriptions, and indeed we know that it stretches as far back as Egyptian sculpture and as far afield as the Japanese print. The ordinary label by which most paintings and statues are accompanied is only another form of the same expedient, here external to the design.

The second and more serious of the common types of ultra-pictorial extension arises in connection with action. Its elements being fixed and motionless, a picture or a statue can, of course, represent only one moment in the sequence of an action. Like a snapshot, it arrests that action at a given instant and fixes it there. The instant chosen is usually an intrinsically significant one and in many cases we are content to contemplate it without curiosity concerning its antecedent phases or its suggested outcome. In other cases, the full significance of the action may not be clear to us from the pictorial instant and we find ourselves requiring further, and again external, explanation. Particularly is this likely to be so in the case of works illustrating history or legend. We may take Millais' "Lorenzo and Isabella" (Fig. 14) as an example.

In contemplating this picture, we observe the attentions being paid to the lady in the right foreground by the man sitting next to her, the apparent displeasure and interference of the man opposite to her, the subtly reserved observation which the men beyond him are directing toward the two characters first mentioned, and the seeming remoteness of the remaining characters from any concern beyond that of finishing their meal. A certain tenseness dominates the scene, charging it with vague suspense and dramatic portent, and there is considerable formal significance in the relations of unity, contrast, and emphasis between the three or four main themes into which the total action subdivides itself.

But these intrinsic pictorial values of the action are not enough to satisfy all the impulses which the picture starts in us. We feel that we cannot fully grasp the situation. We want some further clue as to precisely what is happening. We can secure such a clue only by reference to the further development of the story of which the picture arrests an instant. Again the work stirs impulses which it cannot itself satisfy and in this case full comprehension of its meaning, hence full perception of any associative significance attained through that meaning, demands the satisfaction of those impulses. In this respect it may properly be called "literary" in the narrower and ultra-pictorial sense. It is an example of that type of work which is currently described as "mere illustration."

Thus it would appear that a distinction can be drawn between those extensive sources of associative effect which can be fully rendered in visual art and certain additional effects, particularly those which deal with the identification of objects or characters and the sequence of action, which cannot be fully rendered and which, if they are attempted at all, carry us beyond the limits of painting and sculpture into literature. And it would be further natural to suppose that this distinction could be formulated into the critical principle already quoted and used as an indication of the limit up to which associative effects may properly be carried in visual art and beyond which they cease to be legitimate.

In its positive aspect, this principle undoubtedly represents a considerable measure of truth, though I am not prepared to say that ultra-

FIG. 14. MILLAIS. LORENZO AND ISABELLA
Walker Art Gallery, Liverpool

pictorial extensions can have *no* bearing upon æsthetic experience. To apprehend the woman in our Titian as the Madonna, one of the children as Christ, may add an outer fringe of meaning which enlarges the associative significance of the work in an æsthetic way and which was, in fact, a part of Titian's original conception for the work. The ultra-pictorial meaning, in this case, brings overtones of dignity and impressiveness which echo the underlying pictorial music, extending its harmonies faintly into an ethereal zone beyond the actual pictorial atmosphere. But whatever æsthetic amplification may result from these sources is slight as compared with the effect produced by the underlying plastic and associative elements.

It is also exceptional. For the most part, labels, identities, are purely informative and in no way modify or add to the æsthetic significance of the work which they accompany. Their function is religious, historical, or biographical rather than æsthetic and they represent a demand imposed upon art by those who saw in it other than artistic uses. Whether a Titian portrait be labelled "Jacopo Sannazaro" or, its identity being lost, "Portrait of a Man," does not affect its intrinsic value as a plastic creation or as a character study. Biographical identity may possibly make the work more interesting; it cannot render it more beautiful.

Neither does our acquaintance with the action sequence which a work illustrates modify the degree of significance attained in the representation of the pictorial moment of that action. It may in some cases be necessary to the comprehension of that action—a point to which we shall revert shortly—but it does not enlarge the internal achievement of that action when comprehended. To one who knows nothing about the life of Christ, an "Agony in the Garden" or a

"Crucifixion" will doubtless present mystifying features. The facts of the life of Christ, on the other hand, give no clue to the relative æsthetic excellence of such works. A hundred "Crucifixions" will all be based upon the same facts yet no two of them will be alike in æsthetic value, nor will familiarity with the narrative be the factor which has enabled certain of the artists to create superior works or which will enable an observer to recognize the superior ones when they have been created. In short, the fundamental æsthetic significance of a work of art must always be judged in terms of qualities which are embodied in its internal structure; qualities which ultra-pictorial extensions rarely affect at all and never greatly. To this extent the principle which we have been examining will stand.

But with regard to its further implications, or what at first glance appear to be its implications, this principle may be very misleading. We must proceed cautiously before accepting it in its negative aspect; before asserting, in other words, that no work which involves projections into ultra-pictorial meanings can be æsthetically a significant work and that subject-matter which introduces such projections is by that fact shown to be improper for treatment in visual art. A number of important considerations would seem to refute any such sweeping assumption.

We are obliged to recognize, in the first place, that the degree to which any given meaning can be conveyed by purely visual means, the degree to which it remains independent of external informative devices or "literary" explanation, is not purely a matter of objective relation between the given medium and the given subject-matter. It is conditioned by two additional factors: the conception which the artist has chosen to follow in executing the work and subjective elements in the observer.

When I analyze my experience of the El Greco "Agony," I am surprised to discover how considerably my response to the picture depends upon ultra-pictorial considerations. I *know* rather than *see* that the disciples are sleeping, that the soldiers are approaching to take Christ captive, that the cup symbolizes the necessity of accepting a torturous death. And it is partly as a result of knowing these things that I read into the picture the poignant drama which I feel it to express. Were I completely ignorant of the circumstances, and so dependent entirely upon what I observe in the picture itself, the situation might appear quite otherwise to me and my perception of the whole form would take a correspondingly different "set."

But we must not assume that because the work involves ultra-pictorial extensions, the situation represented was incapable of internal fulfilment in a painting. Had it been the artist's desire to render that situation more fully comprehensible by internal pictorial means, he could easily have done so. Perugino, in fact, has made the sleeping and the approaching much more explicit. Were internal clarity the aim, a version could easily be worked out which would make the situation clear to the most uninformed. I recall a romantic picture of some redskins surrounding a sleeping girl, which left no doubt in any one's mind as to the full significance of the action! But El Greco obviously felt it unnecessary to be explicit about a matter which he knew to be common knowledge. He assumed familiarity with the life of Christ on the part of his observers, and consequently felt himself free to select those aspects of the situation which appealed to him and to represent them as he chose. Thus the degree to which a work possesses internal completeness often depends more largely upon the artist's choice of treatment than it does upon the nature of the subject treated.

In the second place, what we have been calling internal clarity is by no means as "internal" as it seems. It is largely subjective, depending upon the observer's mental development and cultural background—upon the range and adequacy of his "funded experience." The "Lorenzo and Isabella" mystifies us only in proportion to our ignorance of Florentine history. Any one who had participated in the actual episode of Lorenzo and Isabella as an event in real life, or who had otherwise become familiar with the facts of their case, would take in the full dramatic import of the picture at first glance, without recourse to any explanation or "program." He would still be resorting in part to knowledge gained through extra-visual experience, but would do so automatically and subconsciously; hence the picture would seem to him entirely pictorial. He would find it fully self-contained in its meaning and would see no need for supplementing it by any external explanation.

It may be objected that in the presence of a work of visual art we should not be required to *know* anything; that the painter and sculptor should merely invite us to *see*. "In so far as the spectator . . . must depend upon the resources of his own knowledge . . . the effect is illegitimate." Whether such a position can be seriously maintained is doubtful. Carried out to its logical conclusion, it would force us back once more upon second-stratum geometrical design, upon pure decoration, for third-stratum plastic effects and fourth-stratum associative effects all depend to one degree or another upon our "knowing."

We cannot apprehend the splendid stability of an Egyptian sphinx, the mountainous weight of the "Cumean Sybil," unless we "know" what stability and weight are; unless we have "funded" many experiences with them to enrich the associations which they awaken in us. We cannot distinguish the head of the sphinx from its tail, or even be aware of the existence of such things as heads or tails, unless we "know" the salient features of animal anatomy. Leaving aside the question of who the Cumean sybil may have been, we cannot recognize hers as a human form or perceive its individuality as a unique human form, unless we "know" the lineaments and natural variations of humanity. Present a picture to an observer who literally "knows" nothing, that is to say to a new-born child or a total imbecile, and the resulting perception will be of no more than a substance with marks on it—no more, that is to say, than is actually and physically present. Anything not physically present in a work of art must be a mental interpretation of something that is, and mental interpretation is possible only up to the limit of the observer's "knowledge."

Ordinarily we are not conscious of resort to our knowledge in interpreting works of art because, like so many other mental processes, that of interpretation is a spontaneous and subconscious one. We become aware of it only when it is arrested: we realize the function of knowledge only when forced, by some unusual circumstance, to recognize the embarrassment of ignorance. Subjects requiring external explanation are, in fact, little more than subjects with which we happen to be unfamiliar. And to call such subjects "illegitimate" is merely to assert that no artist has a right to express any meanings of which we happen to be ignorant. The position reduces itself to absurdity. There is, in short, no special type of subject-matter or effect which can rationally be debarred from art on the grounds of the distinction between "knowledge" and "vision." On those grounds, as already suggested, we should have to bar everything but geometrical pattern.

Possibly it will be said that although all higher pictorial significance does involve the expression of meanings which must be known in experience before they can be expressed in art, not all meanings are equally appropriate for artistic expression. With this thought in mind, a distinction has sometimes been drawn between *universal* meanings, which are the common possession of all normal human beings, and *particular* meanings which depend upon circumstances unfamiliar to most persons and consequently unintelligible to them. Art, it might seem, may properly incorporate the universal meanings, but it should avoid the particular ones.

This distinction between the universal and the particular, in the sense of the widely and the infrequently experienced, is a serviceable one in certain respects, but it can hardly be employed as a standard upon which to exclude ultra-pictorial meanings from visual art. Given sets of meanings rise and fall in universality with the passage of time, and the artist can hardly be expected to limit himself to those which he supposes may be current at some distant period of history. During the Renaissance, the meanings involved in Christian legend and classical mythology were universal in the community which the artist wished to address. Today they have dwindled to a position not far from the particular. The average observer is no more likely to know who Joachim was or what se:.. him downcast to the sheepfold, than what transpired between Lorenzo and Isabella. His acquaintance with Diana is likely to be slight, with Actæon slighter, and his ignorance of what transpired between them complete. Yet should Giotto have refrained from representing Joachim because later generations would be ignorant of the events connected with the life of the Virgin? Should Titian and his fellows have resisted the inspiration to their pageants of mythology because those same generations would let go their heritage of ancient visions?

There are many outside Europe and America who would be as puzzled by a scene from the life of Christ as most of our western contemporaries are by one representing Joachim. Indeed, generations are not unlikely to arise which will find it as difficult to understand the circumstances of a Seurat "Cirque" or a Renoir "Moulin de la Galette" as do the masses of today a scene from faded legend. To restrict meanings to a genuinely universal sphere would be to reduce them to a very low denominator indeed. More widespread and permanent intelligibility might be insured by so doing, but there would be an enormous loss in the range of material available for art, in the variety of creative problems, and in the stimulus of expressing those meanings which are felt most deeply by the community of which the artist forms a part and for which, in the first instance, he works. The Renaissance artist might have remained clearer to his distant admirers if he had restricted himself as nearly as possible to the universal, but he would have appeared unprofitable to himself and to his contemporaries at a time when visions of the Virgin and Diana were what men lived by.

It is, of course, true that in significant works of art the artist who presents a particular theme succeeds in giving it a universal significance. It will always be the underlying universal meanings rather than the particular and more superficial ones that determine the degree of associative value to which a work attains. From the æsthetic point of view, Joachim's identity and the circumstances of his visit to the sheepfold are incidental to the dramatic human situation which Giotto has represented in terms of them. But this merely indicates that the exclusion of the particular is far from being the surest road to the achievement of the universal. Often the artist achieves the greatest universality when he is most fully absorbed in the individualistic and, it may be, partially ultra-pictorial subject.

Quite apart from these theoretical considerations, we might well be discouraged from any attempt to bar ultra-pictorial extensions from art by the array of great work which involves them. As already implied by many of the examples cited, such extensions are by no means peculiar to popular romantic art of the type represented by the "Lorenzo and Isabella." They are common to nine-tenths of what we esteem the great art of the world. We should have to wipe out nearly the whole production of the Renaissance if we determined to eradicate them, and then pursue our inquisitory activities through nearly all periods and schools, oriental as well as occidental, from ancient up to modern times.

These constantly recurring ultra-pictorial extensions represent the transitional zone between the experience of visual art and that of other phases of culture; a zone in which all the arts overlap in their common service to those impulses which are deepest in the life of the community from which the artist emerges and for which he speaks. Giotto, Titian, El Greco, undoubtedly considered it good fortune that art was thus able to embody the things that mattered most to their respective societies. They would have had difficulty, I imagine, in understanding why it should wish to do otherwise than profit by the advantage thus opened to it. They knew that their essential artistic concern lay with vision, but they also knew that social inspiration, far from interfering with vision, stimulates and enriches it. Only in a period of great sophistication and self-consciousness, or one not sure of its artistic aims, or one swayed by scientific experimentation, could it occur to an artist that his work should be exclusively visual; that is to say, deliberately severed from the thoughts and feelings dominant in his community. And even in a period in which that thought arises, its influence is not likely to be prolonged or far-reaching, as modern art itself testifies. The production of today, significant as well as insignificant, is full of ultra-pictorial bonds with current thought and feeling, bonds which we ourselves hardly recognize because they are so intimately a part of life as we accept it. To the future, they will stand out clearly.

Indeed, we may remark parenthetically that that phase of modern art which seems furthest from ultra-pictorial concerns, namely that which has experimented with abstract form, will probably impress future observers less by its form than by its social expressiveness. Formally, it will be in no sense unique, for all significant art has form and the great formal achievements of the past surpass in richness and beauty any that have been left by the abstractionists. As we have seen elsewhere, abstraction has proved to be a limitation rather than a help so far as concerns the ultimate possibilities of visual form. In the long run, therefore, the striking thing about abstract art will not be the beauty of form in which it has been so frequently surpassed, but the abstractness which is to be found nowhere else. And that abstractness, the logical outcome of a theory favored by scientific and mechanical thought, will be seen as a manifestation, and felt as an expression, of social forces strong in twentieth-century culture. Thus by one of the strange reversals of time, that art which most abjured expression for form will see its form strongly colored, perhaps dominated, by expression. Such art will "date" as surely as a colonial sampler and will doubtless show forth a historical quaintness as unmistakable and as charming.

We should note further that these same abstract schools which did most, in their short ascendancy, to unsettle the traditional attitude toward subject-matter, were often the ones whose work involved the most positive "literary" and ultra-pictorial developments that modern art has witnessed. Cubism, Futurism, Synchronism, all had their start more largely in ideas than in immediate visual stimulus. The Cubist theory of resolving an object into its constituent planes and reassembling them in the interests of design was a *con*ception rather than a *per*ception; a principle rather than a vision. And as we know, most of the ultra-modern groups have issued their pronouncements and explanations, in a word, their "programs."

If the "Lorenzo and Isabella" is insignificant as a work of visual art, then, this is not because of the ultra-pictorial elements which it shares in common with much of the great art of the past and the significant art of the present. It is rather because it lacks other qualities which such art possesses. We must seek elsewhere than in the literary fringe of visual art for the qualities which determine its visual significance.

We have now reached the point at which we can summarize the results of the inquiry to which the present chapter has been devoted; an inquiry aiming to determine how far associative effects are legitimate in visual art. If we have analyzed the matter rightly, none of the charges which have been raised against them will stand. Their relation to the focus of attention is no different from that of the plastic elements; they merely extend and enrich the perceptive continuum, and no more compete with plastic effects than such effects compete with each other. They are extra-visual only in the same degree as third-stratum plastic effects. They are not "literary" except in the sense that literature may create similar effects, for they arise spontaneously in the artist's experience of the visual universe and would be embodied in painting and sculpture whether literature existed or not.

Different aspects of subject-matter do, however, differ in their seeming "internal completeness" and, more genuinely, in their relative universality. The more internal and universal meanings constitute the essential resources of æsthetic effect which associative elements confer upon visual art. The more external and particular ones constitute an emanation from visual elements into an ultra-pictorial zone and make little positive contribution to visual art. But their presence is not necessarily detrimental to the value of such art. That value depends upon other factors. And from the creative point of view, the acceptance of subjects involving ultra-pictorial extensions has greatly increased the range of material available to art and the variety of problems encountered in producing it. The increased materials have enriched art; the accompanying problems have stimulated vital creative effort and furthered significant production.

Thus we reach the conclusion that no basis for discrediting associative elements can be found. They are as native to painting and sculpture, as legitimate there, as any other elements. And they make contributions, some direct, some indirect, without which visual art cannot reach maximum æsthetic effect. The essential question to be considered, therefore, is not whether representational art should accept the associative effects potential to its representational elements, but what the proper place of such effects is in a work of visual art as a whole:

how important they are as compared with the underlying and equally native plastic effects and in what manner the two are related to each other. In order to answer this question, and so to judge the ultimate place of associative effects in visual art, we must next study the relationships existing between those two main sources of æsthetic value which thus far we have considered in isolation from each other: plastic and associative form.

CHAPTER VIII

REPRESENTATIONAL FORM

The conception of associative form presented in an earlier chapter involves relatively little that is new. Character and action have always been recognized as forms in literature and the discussion of their relative unities and amplitudes is common practice in literary criticism. In the field of visual art, eighteenth-century critics had considered subject-matter from an æsthetic point of view and had perceived its relation to form, though they do not seem to have recognized that it might itself *be* form. Later, Santayana and others assisted in extending critical concepts first evolved for literature by giving them their proper place in general æsthetics.

Still more recently, as mentioned in our introductory chapter, M. Charles Mauron conceived by analogy with the tangible volumes of plastic art, the "psychological volumes" which he felt might explain the æsthetic appeal of literature, and Mr. Fry in turn found in this conception of psychological volumes a key to the potential æsthetic significance of subject-matter in visual art. Apart from the change in the name, our discussion has involved little not already found in Mr. Fry's study of "psychological form," unless it be a more explicit analysis of the elements giving rise to such form and a choice of examples less uniquely "literary" and hence more characteristic of representational effects as found in the best visual art.

But Mr. Fry's analysis leads him to the conclusion that associative and plastic forms are so distinct from each other as to imply two separate arts, and that when painting or sculpture seeks to combine them, it becomes, like the opera, a compound art. He finds further that the relation of these two sources of effect to each other is one of inverse ratios, and that the greater the "psychological" significance, the less must be the plastic significance, if conflict between the two is to be avoided. Our analysis has been leading us toward a different conclusion.

Let us now address ourselves to this final problem: that of the relationship existing between plastic and associative form. The earlier steps of our discussion have prepared the way for us. We have found that representation enters visual art through concurrences of the object-recalling associations which all visual or plastic elements awaken. This much alone would seem to disprove Mr. Fry's theory of a compound art, for we perceive at once that there is only one medium present. We do not have visual elements and language or some other independent source of effect brought together, as the opera brings music and language together. We have nothing but visual elements. Representation is one sphere of effect potential to such elements without recourse to any additional medium.

Representational art might be more truly compared to program music, where the purely musical sounds convey impressions of things or events, were it not for the fact that only in a few exceptional cases, such as bird songs, thunder, or the stirring of winds and waters, can the desired context be directly suggested by the music. Usually it must be provided for the listener by an accompanying verbal explanation. No such explanation is necessary in the case of representational art, at least so far as concerns its basic æsthetic values. If we want to know *who* a given character is, for instance, we have crossed the border between the central æsthetic sphere and one of its ultra-pictorial extensions. But the essential æsthetic consideration of how vividly that character is represented, how significant the character-form, can be determined—*must* be determined—by visual observation of the form constructed for us in the picture.

Representational painting and sculpture are, therefore, most nearly akin to poetry, in which words having in their first stratum an abstract or "musical" basis, words capable of being woven into beautiful patterns of pure sound, are not delimited exclusively as sounds but project their significance into related realms of meaning and there make possible additional strata of æsthetic effect. Poetry is hardly to be regarded as a compound art simply because it involves abstract as well as representational, "musical" as well as "literary," elements. It is indeed—and sculpture and painting like it—a complex art, one involving several possible strata of effect within its single medium. In this sense, if we wished to call attention to the component spheres of effect within the total form of any of the representational arts, it might be convenient to describe that form as "compound." But that would be giving the term a narrower and very different meaning from the accepted one which Mr. Fry employs and which he illustrates by reference to the combination of separate media in the opera.

Again reverting to the earlier stages of our discussion, we recall that plastic elements possess a power of awakening expressive over-tones quite independently of the more sharply focussed associations which lead to object-suggestion or representation. Thus colors, as such, may evoke moods of gayety, exaltation, serenity, dignity; lines may assume traits of animation or repose, of masculine strength or feminine suppleness. It is here that we find the æsthetic link between plastic and associative elements; here that we find the precise nature of what Doctor Barnes has called "plastic equivalents." Associative effects involve similar, though usually more fully crystallized, expressive vibrations. Characters also may be gay or dignified, masculine or feminine; actions may be animated, languorous, or serene. Thus it becomes possible for the artist to create varied blendings of plastic and representational expressiveness; to choose the color that harmonizes with the character, the line that vibrates in sympathy with the action; to extend yet once more his web of relationships by relating plastic foundations and their associative superstructures, and in so doing, once more to enrich and amplify his form.

That such interrelations of plastic and associative elements give rise to form is evident, since they are organized relationships. And this form can now properly be called neither plastic nor associative, since it combines elements from both these spheres. It would have to be called plastic-associative form. More conveniently and with equal fitness we may term it simply "representational" form, for in its combination of plastic with associative elements, it constitutes the governing and the typical form in representational art. Similarly, in speaking of sculpture or painting individually, we might call it "sculptural" or "pictorial" form, for it is the typical form of each of these arts in particular as of representational art in general. Plastic and associative forms, considered individually, are merely components of this total representational form. Indeed, when seen in their component function, they lose their individual boundaries and merge into one final network of relations, which embraces the work of art as a whole and which constitutes the farthest limit to which form can be pressed in representational art; the farthest limit indeed (architecture always excluded from present consideration) to which it can be carried within the visual world.

The examples which we have already used for their associative effects will serve further to illustrate the more inclusive relations between those effects and their plastic accompaniments. Let us begin our observations with the first Rembrandt "Old Woman" (Fig. 9). What type of color and what qualities of illumination has Rembrandt brought into relationship with the character which we observed as the dominant source of associative effect?

The color scheme is worked out largely in restrained golden browns —colors of a type that we find in things old and seasoned and that we frequently describe as "mellow." The illumination is one suggestive of dusk—softly glowing highlights in a world of shadow; an illumination dominantly somber, yet with a glow in its shadows and with a mellow richness in its lights. Thus the color and light are of a nature which in their turn evoke impressions of mellowness; which bring with them expressive overtones of aging and seasoning, of evening here and night not far away. What other colors, what other light, could blend so perfectly with the character represented? What harmony could be richer, softer, subtler or more solemn in its reverberations, than the harmony which Rembrandt achieves through this blending? No more significant relationship, none more varied in the range of its component notes, none more seemingly inevitable in the affinity of those notes for each other, could be established within the whole realm of vision. Imagine this character in conjunction with dazzling color and shimmering light, imagine it accompanied by the plastic brilliance of a late Renoir or a Matisse—we perceive at once how the harmony would vanish, like fairies at the approach of boisterous intruders, and how incongruity and discord would replace it. The unity of the embracing pictorial form would be broken, the observer's delight in exquisitely organized relations cut short, the enjoyment of an æsthetic experience replaced by irritation or indifference.

Other examples which it is illuminating to compare with our Rembrandt because of their application of the same principle to entirely different sets of relations, may be found in the dashing brushwork and at times exuberant color which Franz Hals brings into relation with jovial types of character; the sobriety of plastic effect, the nicety of composition, which Titian relates to his patrician sitters; the serpentine line and subtle haunting combination of blue-green and yellowish and reddish brown which Leonardo works into relation with the enigmatic personality of his "Mona Lisa." To find the plastic equivalent of joviality or nobility, to compound the plastic enigma, that is one of the most elusive and one of the most fascinating problems to which the artist can devote himself.

And just as the final form of the work would be less rich without the added relations that result from this organizing of expressive overtones, the final expressiveness of the work would be less compelling without the reinforcement of the subject-matter by the expressiveness of appropriate plastic accompaniments. The depth of characterization which gives universality to our Rembrandt "Old Woman," compressing into it the distilled essence of all old age and of a whole range of human life, does not reside exclusively in its representational elements. Taken in isolation, those elements could stir only a portion of the response we feel before the original work. It is those elements backed by, echoed by, amplified by, the accompanying color, light, and breadth of surface, which produce the full expressive vibration and stir us so deeply. Expression provides the germinating motif, the point of departure, for the form and brings with it multiple elements for the enrichment of the form. The form gives power and profundity to the expression, conferring upon it that "reality" which attends all textures of significantly organized relations and which indeed, even for philosophy and science, seems to have no existence apart from them.

Further examples can add nothing to the principle thus illustrated, but a brief examination of our Titian and our El Greco will enable us to extend that principle to works involving a larger number of elements and thus giving rise to more complex and varied total relations. The Titian "Madonna of the Cherries" (Fig. 11) has one associative element in common with the Rembrandt just considered: a certain serious and spiritual quality. Appropriately enough it also has one color quality in common with the Rembrandt, a quality definitely related to seriousness; the quality we frequently call "richness." The color is deep and restrained, somber in parts, weighted everywhere by its saturation with gold. But beyond this effect of richness, it follows a different course. Browns would unnecessarily limit the splendor of these heavenly beings. Reds, blues, greens appear, subdued by the dominant richness, but creating an effect of restrained magnificence— plastic equivalent of the restrained exaltation involved in the religious conception of the scene. Richness of texture contributes to the same effect, making these figures seem patrician, and the stern-textured saints of Tura and Roberti ascetic in comparison.

As we should expect, there is less shadow and more light than in the Rembrandt and a quality of light less of the dusk and more of tempered sunshine. Furthermore, gradation of light and color, from their highest intensity on the Madonna and Child to their lowest on the two male saints, is the chief means by which the artist has attained the scale of emphasis already noted as a phase of the character relations. Thus an *associative* emphasis is attained by a *plastic* gradation. What could illustrate more clearly the interdependence of these two spheres of effect? It is true that the gradation of light and color, and the use to which it is put in building up and varying the plastic design, holds great beauty purely as a plastic achievement. But its full significance does not appear if we consider it exclusively as a plastic phenomenon. Its disposition is determined by, and its full significance must be observed in relation to, associative elements. Its present relation to the several characters enriches the total representational form, just as an inverse relation to those same characters—light on the side figures and shadow on the central ones—would strain that form with uncoördinated relations.

Finally, let us note the relation of the general plastic pattern, the particular type of "composition," to the subject-matter. Approaching the firm balance of symmetry, with a broadly based triangle buttressed by lateral masses, the design is one of which dignity, stability, and a definite clearly determined order are the chief expressive attributes. No attributes could fit better with a theme which aims at religious poise and meditative calm. Thus plastic and associative qualities merge with each other through their common overtones, and the harmony between the two component networks within the embracing total form is complete and many-sided.

The El Greco (Fig. 12) sets a different problem. Dramatic intensity and tragic stress are its associative keynotes. What effects of color and plastic design has El Greco sought out to vibrate in harmony with them? The color, for the most part is dreary and forbidding, coming to a focal point of gloom in the rock behind Christ, which is a cold stony gray. Dull greens, pale blues, and other cool impersonal colors rise to yellow-green and yellow in the angel, reaching there a note of urgency but not of cheer. Only in the blue robe and red mantle of Christ do we find appealing notes suggestive of human warmth and sensitivity.

These various colors are so arranged on the canvas that the strongest and warmest notes in the robe of Christ come immediately in front of the most dismal ones in the rock, and that there is a circular progression from the dullness of the rock, through rising intensities and increasing warmth of hues in the main vista, the foreground, and the angel, to a climax in the robes of Christ; a climax immediately engulfed each time we reach it by the background of surrounding gloom. The whole drama of the subject-matter is echoed in the minor strains of this color music. Human suffering in an inhuman world; the inexorable cycle of hopelessness and resignation rising periodically, like a beating heart, to the warmth of hope and then caught back once more into the gray of despair. El Greco has pursued to their ultimate development and woven together into the organized relations of an art form, the subtle affinities between colors and human emotions. He has carried out in visual terms and with the skill of a great artist what the common man senses when he describes unhappy days as "gray" or dispirited moods as "blue."

A similar aptness to the central motif appears in the delineation, and in the restless, flame-like treatment of the light. A swirling movement characterizes the design, a movement like that with which the world reels when one grows dizzy and is near to fainting. Furthermore, the space is compressed largely into the immediate foreground, where, with the exception of the path closed by the soldiers and the hopeless reaches into upper darkness, it is walled in by the close-pressing rocks, clouds, and other objects. Plastic equivalent of confinement, of the impossibility of escape, of life focussed by intense feeling upon the plane of immediate all-absorbing experience.

Thus we have in the picture, plastically through color, linear movement, and imprisoned space as well as associatively in the setting previously discussed, a visualization of the world as it would seem to one in the position of Christ; an objectification of the experience to which such a person would be subject; a fusion of outer and inner meanings; a fusion, in other words, of all the aspects of experience represented in and afforded by the picture; a network of interwoven relations to which no single quality of the work, sensuous, formal, or expressive, is extraneous; a unified, richly nourished, and wonderfully organized representational *form*.

In these respects, as well as in its associative conception, the Perugino version (Fig. 13) offers an illuminating basis of comparison. I do not recall the original and cannot speak certainly of its colors. But if they are typical of their author, they are presumably of a pleasant and rather tranquil quality, a serene blue being characteristic among them. If such be the colors, it is apparent that they contribute to a calm and meditative effect and have no bearing upon the theme of the present work. Furthermore, as we can see in the reproduction, the design is a quiet and well poised one, of which placid rhythms and an easy balance are the chief constituents, while the background opens into serene distance and unrestricted space, allowing the spirit an avenue of escape into oblivion. In none of these respects do the plastic aspects of the work harmonize with, or reinforce, the motif set by its subject.

It may be objected to these criticisms that Perugino has chosen to give that motif a calmer and more lyric development, and that the plastic qualities which he employs harmonize with the equivalently less dramatic associative treatment. The artist, it may be said, is at liberty to give a theme his personal interpretation; to lyricize it, if he will, as well as to dramatize it. So much is true and it must be granted that there is a considerable degree of coherence between certain elements of the Perugino version. But its coherence is not complete. A dramatic motif is the point of departure for the work; there are a limited number of dramatic inventions in its execution. Dramatic and lyric effects divide it, preventing the fusion of all its elements into a unified form, and creating a conflict between the dominantly dramatic nature of the theme and the dominantly lyric nature of its representation. In the El Greco all fuses, all reinforces; form is complete and indivisible and by its complete dedication to the central motif carries that motif forward to an ultimate expression.

A hundred fascinating studies suggest themselves when we begin to investigate art-forms in the light of the principle we have been considering. Giotto's use of line for the reinforcement of subject-matter would in itself provide material for an essay. How he roots it where immobility is needed, droops it when the mood falls to sadness, draws it into close harmonies at moments of tenderness, sends it forward or backward to create the impression of movement or recoil! Our whole thesis is resumed in the contrast between the limpid harmonies of the

"Meeting of Joachim and Anna" and the linear discords and confusion of another meeting—that of Jesus with his assailants in the scene of his arrest on Gethsemane. And how splendidly, apart from lines, the monumental simplicity of Giotto's plastic conception reinforces the nobility of his subject-matter. Alone of later Renaissance painters, Michelangelo achieved a similar monumentality. He achieved it because he needed it to reinforce the epic drama of his subject-matter. Or, more accurately, that subject-matter, in his hands, rose to the plane of epic drama because its associative grandeur was reinforced by the grandeur of plastic monumentality.

Other illuminating perceptions will come to the observer who studies the different types of design in a series of works by Titian having different types of subject. Although there are, of course, certain plastic qualities common, in a general way, to all his work, so great an artist neither repeats his designs uncreatively nor invents them indiscriminately without reference to their associative ingredients. If the firmly based pyramid is one equation for the poise of a Madonna, the thrust becomes unstable—sideward and uphill—to accompany the spiritual striving of a St. Jerome; the lines are drooping and solicitous in the "Entombment," while in the "Venus and Adonis," the composition pulses with the movement of a whirlpool and shimmers in a flood of iridescent light.

Indeed, so obvious is the relation which Titian establishes between his plastic and his associative effects that we can hardly concur, nor does it seem that Titian himself would have concurred, with the full implication of a comparison made by Doctor Barnes and already mentioned above. I refer to the plate on which the Titian "Entombment" and a Cézanne "Still-Life" are brought together with the comment:

"The design of these two paintings is very similar, showing irrelevancy of subject-matter to plastic value." That the type of subject-matter involved in a work does not determine its plastic value is evident; is in fact true irrespective of similarities of design. But that, in significant art, the type of subject-matter has no relation to the type of plastic value developed to accompany it, may be seriously questioned.

In point of fact the design of the two paintings in question is similar only in a limited sense. There is indeed a similarity of linear pattern and a partial similarity in the placement of color "values." But in many significant plastic respects, the two works are quite dissimilar. This becomes evident if we compare them with regard to intensity of color, quality of illumination, relative amount of shadow, and relation of weighing masses to their supports and to the intervening voids. Nor can there be any doubt that the particular effects of color, illumination, and mass, as well as the nature of the linear design, employed by Titian have a definite bearing upon the subject-matter which he is representing. In the case of the Cézanne, associative elements play a very minor rôle. Hence the design is less influenced by them and more largely self-determined as a plastic creation. That it should possess a disposition of parts in common with the Titian proves little more, in this case, than that such a disposition is plastically a significant one and therefore not unlikely to recur wherever plastic design is pursued.

As may be seen by reference to our plates, the Cézanne "Mt. Ste. Victoire," the Titian "Madonna of the Cherries," and the El Greco "Agony" also have a general disposition of parts in common, namely that of a dominating central triangle. In each case that triangle creates an effect of stability, an effect which bears a definite relation to some aspect of the accompanying subject-matter. But such partial similarities are far from total similarities and far from proving what the plate under discussion would seem to imply.

Many additional examples of the interrelation between plastic and associative elements will occur to the reader if he reflects upon the plastic qualities which accompany, and help to create, the combination of midsummer calm and autumn melancholy in Giorgione, the drama of Tintoretto and Rubens, the mystical ecstasy which is even more characteristic of El Greco than the dramatic tension of his "Agony," the exuberant lyricism of Renoir, or the legendary remoteness of Puvis de Chavannes. Nor must we forget that within the more limited range permitted by the medium, the same principle applies to sculpture. Where, without their underlying plastic qualities, would be the eternal calm of the Egyptian gods and pharaohs, the majesty of the Parthenon "Fates," the resolute firmness of Donatello's "St. George," or the dramatic power of Verocchio's "Colleoni"?

A subject so fascinating tempts one to pursue it further, but we have already carried it to the limits compatible with our general study of form and representation. We have seen that plastic and associative elements, each a potential source of formal beauty in themselves, in turn meet each other to create new relations and so give rise to an embracing plastic-associative, or representational, form. Such form, woven of all the elements perceptible to vision and of all the overtones which those elements are capable of awakening in our consciousness, integrating in its fabric every ramification of experience which visual stimuli can start in us, is at once the richest and loftiest form into which visual elements can be built and the source of the greatest æsthetic delight which painting and sculpture can afford.

CHAPTER IX

REPRESENTATIONAL FORM: ASPECTS AND
VARIATIONS

Our study has now led us to the general conclusion that plastic, associative, and plastic-associative relations are essential to maximum formal effect in visual art. To say that they are all essential to this effect, however, is not equivalent to saying that they are all equally significant within it, or that, in isolation, any one of these sets of relations is equal in potential æsthetic value to any other. It remains to consider this final question of the relative part played by each of these component networks of relations in the total form—a question raised but left unanswered at the close of our discussion of the legitimacy of associative effects.

In answering it we shall be able to consider certain reservations concerning our general position which the reader may still feel himself obliged to make. For most critical observers, I doubt not, will find it necessary to maintain that whatever part may be credited to associative effects in visual art, plastic effects are nevertheless more fundamental there, and that creations of an exclusively "literary" type, like our "Lorenzo and Isabella," do not justify consideration as significant works of art at all. In order to establish our position as firmly, and at the same time to define it as exactly as possible, we shall do well to examine it in the light of these reservations, and also to test it with reference to certain types of art not yet considered—among others the partially significant but "melodramatic" work of Delacroix to which reference was made in our opening section.

An approach to the question of the relative importance of plastic and associative effects can be made in terms of what may be called the principle of "priority." We have seen, in the course of our earlier analysis, that representation results from concurrences of the object-suggesting associations of plastic elements. It is thus a kind of super-structure dependent upon underlying plastic foundations or, to change the image, an outer sphere of effect dependent upon emanations from a plastic center. Plastic effects up to certain limits can exist without associative emanations, but associative effects cannot exist without plastic foundations. Thus the plastic elements are in some sense basic, while the associative elements are derivative.

This might seem to be enough to give the plastic elements the dominant place among the sources of æsthetic value in visual art. But comparison with other types of art indicates that this principle is by no means absolute. Sound is similarly more basic in literature than is meaning, for the meaning cannot be evoked except by the sounds which convey it; sounds for which the letters of written language are merely graphic symbols. Yet if the musical elements dependent upon sound (the equivalent of plastic effects in visual art) are more basic in literature, it may nevertheless be doubted whether they play a larger part in determining literary value. Reduced to isolation they are relatively meager in their capacity for form-building, as all attempts at abstract poetry indicate and as may further be determined by listening to poetry in a language which we do not understand. The range of sounds which, first, can be produced by the human voice, and second, can be employed by the voice in speech, and third, can be chosen for use under the conditions imposed by consistency of meaning—only a few sounds being available when any given meaning is required—the range of sounds permitted by these several limitations is relatively slight, hence the potential musical effects are correspondingly simple. Associative elements are thus called upon to play the major part in amplifying literary form.

In music, on the other hand, although we have the same physical medium of sound, just the reverse is true. A great variety of instruments and varied combinations of voices make possible the production of an infinite range of sounds and these sounds, unrestricted by the necessity of concurring with arbitrarily assigned meanings, can be freely employed for their maximum intrinsic significance. Extremely rich and significant musical (abstract) effects are possible under these conditions and associative effects hardly enter pure music at all.

If, then, priority as a physical basis in the given medium is one condition affecting the relative importance of the component spheres of effect in a work of art, it can hardly be the chief condition. Even more influential in determining that importance would seem to be the capacity which the various sources of effect, employed under the conditions of the given art, exhibit for the creation of form. The larger part any given type of element plays in contributing to the formal significance of that art, the more important æsthetically that type of element may be considered in it.

Now we have seen that the plastic elements in visual art, although only intermediate in their capacity for form-building if limited to an abstract status, achieve formal capacities of a high order when given their maximum development through the help of representation. In such work as our Cézanne landscape, for instance, they become a source of profound formal beauty, while associative elements, though present and enjoyable, are of secondary importance. We have also seen that associative elements, when developed by a Rembrandt, a Titian, or an El Greco, may likewise give rise to forms of decided richness and of remarkable subtlety. The range which we saw them attain in our El Greco "Agony" could be considerably extended were we to turn, let us say, to a Tintoretto "Crucifixion" or a Veronese feast scene.

It seems necessary to recognize as a first general principle, therefore, that the representational visual arts occupy more or less of a medial position with regard to the relative place held in them by plastic and associative effects. The plastic effects have infinitely richer possibilities of form-building than do their equivalents in literature, but probably less rich possibilities than their equivalents in music. The associative possibilities are vastly greater than in music, but less great than in literature. Plastic and associative effects are much more nearly equal in potential importance than they are in either literature or music.

If, within this approach to a balance in importance, a still more accurate weighing of the two were desired, we should have to pursue it along the lines of a detailed analysis and comparison of their respective form-building capacities. To undertake this with any pretense at accuracy would call for careful and elaborate study and would lead us beyond the bounds of our present subject. In a previous attempt to determine the principal elements of beauty in visual art, I find that I have attributed approximately eighty significant categories of effect to plastic sources and only about half that number to associative ones. Apart from any attempt at enumeration, my personal feeling of the matter would also suggest that the larger contribution to visual beauty is made by the plastic elements. I believe that the consensus of critical opinion represents a similar finding. Without undertaking an exact demonstration of the case, it seems safe to say in general, then, that the plastic elements must be recognized as in some degree the dominant ones.

Further evidence in support of this conclusion arises when we observe the two spheres of effect in isolation from each other; when, that is, one or the other of them becomes the sole source of æsthetic value in a given work. In this case, physical priority gives the plastic elements a decided advantage. As a result of it, they can be used, in their simpler second-stratum forms, entirely without associative accompaniments. Even in their higher third-stratum developments, they can remain relatively free of such accompaniments, at least in certain types of subject-matter like landscape and still-life. Hence there can be pure (or perfect) forms which are exclusively plastic: forms in which the plastic elements are significantly organized and in which no others are present.

But the converse is not true. As already noted, associative forms cannot exist without plastic foundations. What may exist is a work in which the associative elements alone have been wrought into significant relations; a work the formal significance of which is largely or entirely associative. In such work, the plastic elements constituting the necessary substructure will exist, even though they are not organized. The total form of the work, therefore, will consist of a disorganized mixture of plastic elements bearing an organized network of associative elements. It will be a form broken by large gaps of formlessness. And since the formless areas are those dependent upon the prior, and in that sense more basic, elements—the elements which lie, as it were, closer to the center of existence of a visual object—the work will produce a hollow effect. Its significance will appear as on the surface, or in its outer sphere, while the inner sphere and in some sense the core is discovered to be in a state of disintegration.

The advantage thus gained by the plastic elements when used in isolation has doubtless played a large part in helping to establish the opinion that plastic form is by far the most important, perhaps the sole, source of æsthetic value in visual art. But we must remember with regard to painting and sculpture—which are all that here concern us—that works in which either set of elements appears in isolation are the exceptions rather than the rule. Most great works of representational art involve both spheres of effect. The relative significance of the two in combination is, therefore, a more important matter than their relative significance in isolation.

All points considered, the answer to the question of relative importance seems, in a general way, to involve two main considerations. The plastic elements appear to rank as the dominant ones, chiefly because of their greater capacity for enriching visual form, to a less extent because of their power of producing pure formal effects in isolation from associative accompaniments; perhaps to a slight extent by virtue of the mere fact of their physical priority. But their dominance is far from being an absolute one like that of their equivalents in music. The associative elements also make rich contributions to visual form, so much so that they do not come far behind the plastic ones in importance. They are in fact important enough to suggest an approach to equality, a balancing of plastic and associative effects, as the typical interrelationship in visual art.

The rich potentialities offered by associative effects as well as by plastic ones doubtless account for the fact that in a given series of works, more or less equal in formal significance, there may be considerable differences in the relative importance given to these two component sources of effect. Forms involving relatively little associative development, like the Cézanne "Landscape," forms which involve more or less of a balance between the two, like our Rembrandt "Old Woman," and forms in which associative elements dominate, like Rembrandt's etching of "The Prodigal Son," are all authentic works of art of a high order. The total number of visual elements, plastic and associative, is so extensive that it permits of a considerable variation of emphasis, a considerable choice in the selection of elements to be incorporated in the given work, while still insuring a rich formal achievement.

Let us now consider certain variations of representational form resulting from different combinations of the several component spheres of representational effect. Those excessively "literary" works of which we have taken the "Lorenzo and Isabella" (Fig. 14) as an example, can be accounted for in terms of what has already been said. They belong to that class which depends for its æsthetic significance exclusively upon associative elements. In the modelling of character, in the harmony, contrast, and emphasis of character relations, in the unity of the action and the contrast of its several themes, in the integration of the action with the characters, and the further harmony of the whole with its setting, the "Lorenzo and Isabella" attains considerable formal significance. But there its significance stops. The multiple plastic elements are used without concern for their intrinsic relations; they are introduced only in an auxiliary sense as necessary to the suggestion of objects and through those objects the expression of meanings. The elements employed in the form are organized solely with respect to their meanings and are disorganized with respect to their immediate appearance. As a result, we have one of those "hollow" forms already described.

These facts, I believe, explain the particular emotional responses aroused by art of this type both in the layman and in the cultivated observer. The layman receives a more compelling experience from such art than from almost any other. His contemplative equipment, developed in daily life, consists of an acute perception of meanings and a comparative blindness to plastic values. This equipment functions perfectly in relation to a "Lorenzo and Isabella." Its owner, familiar with meanings, is quick to perceive them and to grasp the relations between them. Oblivious to plastic relations in any case, he fails to perceive their insignificance or disorder in the work before him and so goes away completely satisfied. He has received what is probably the highest æsthetic experience that art can afford him at his stage of development: an experience of form, with its attendant sense of exhilaration and heightened reality, but (without his knowing it) of form that is one-sided and shallow as compared with others of which visual art is capable.

Before this same work, the cultivated observer is likely to feel a mixed response. He is attracted, perhaps in spite of his better critical judgment, and at the same time repelled; attracted most at first glance and repelled the more strongly the longer he remains and the more fully he attempts to satisfy his æsthetic powers. The element of attraction arises from the fact that there is in the work before him an aspect of form. The organized associative relations grip his mind and afford him a first step in formal experience. But there the significant relations stop. Disorder underlies the outer shell of order, and the discord is experienced all the more sharply in contrast to the foretaste and promise of form.

That, I believe, is why art of this type is held up for scorn by the modern critic as the most detestable of all; as not merely insignificant but counterfeit. If it were completely formless it would be harmless enough and would hardly attract even the layman. It pretends to æsthetic significance and indeed possesses a veneer of form, yet is in a large measure formless—it hides a deception behind a pretense— that is its unforgivable sin. And if, because of its shortcoming in this respect, we choose to describe it as "literary," then we must do so with caution. Appropriate enough, as an indication that art of this type is limited to an associative significance, the term is hardly a fortunate one. For the deficiency of such art lies, not in possessing literary elements, which it shares in common with many great works of visual art, but in *not* possessing significant plastic foundations. To indicate its defect accurately, we should have to use some such terms as those suggested above and call it "visual, but hollow at the core."

It may be well in passing to mention two other defective combinations of plastic and associative components. One occurs in works which are plastically significant and which involve marked associative aspects, but which fail to achieve, or consistently to maintain, associative significance. A number of such works were mentioned in our discussion of the legitimacy of associative values. We may recall as typical among them certain Manets in which action and setting appear stilted and artificial. The form of such works is satisfying to a considerable degree, since its plastic foundations are significantly organized. It is solid at the core, but fails of perfection because of blemishes on the surface. Hence the pleasure which it gives us is not likely to be ultimate.

There is also possible a form in which both the plastic and the associative components are significant in their internal organization, but fail to establish unified relations with each other. An instance of this can be found, to my mind, in the Degas "Repasseuses" in the Louvre. Coarse types of character and menial action are brought into relation with color and texture of great delicacy and refinement. A similar plastic effect "fuses" completely with the associative qualities of certain Degas nudes and dancers. In the present work, however, the relationship is a questionable one. We can enjoy both the ethereal plastic form and the rather robust and strident associative form, but to enjoy the one fully we must diminish as much as possible our consciousness of the other. This means that the work lacks certain positive relations which it might possess, while it disturbs our enjoyment of those which it does possess by imposing certain negative relations upon us. The core and the shell are both good, but they do not fit each other properly.

The various degrees of extension possible to visual form and the various interrelations possible between the components of such form, so far as we have now considered them, may be conveniently summarized by graphic means, as indicated in Fig. 15. Suppose that a number of straight lines are taken to represent the second-stratum plastic elements, color, line, shape, and size. If combinations of these elements are brought into organized relationship with each other, we obtain a geometrical pattern, which may be symbolized (and in this case is actually created) by arranging our lines in star formation (*a*). If to these elements are added the third-stratum plastic ones, such as mass and space, and if the relations between these are also organized and are integrated with the already existing second-stratum ones, then our network of relations is amplified and our form correspondingly enriched, as symbolized by (*b*). If, in the same manner, fourth-stratum associative elements are added, organized, and integrated, a further and final enrichment of the form takes place (*c*).

These three diagrams retrace the progression which we have already studied from second through third to fourth-stratum forms. They correspond roughly to the three types of work which were illustrated respectively by our geometrical lace pattern, our Cézanne "Landscape," and any one of our several examples of inclusive representational form, let us say, the El Greco "Agony." It is evident that they differ from each other in amplitude, growing in formal significance with each increase in the number of their component elements, and reaching maximum formal beauty only in (*c*).[1] At the same time (*a*) and (*b*) are also unbroken contexts of relations, organizing all the elements which they possess and thus, up to their respective limits, constituting beautiful forms. Although they do not share the range of (*c*), they equal it in formal perfection.

The reverse is true of the three defective types of work discussed a few pages back. They share the inclusiveness of (*c*), but fail of perfection because of lapses in their organization. In the first type, illustrated by the "Lorenzo and Isabella," the plastic elements are used as a necessary substratum to associative effects, but without consideration

[1] The use of the Cézanne as an example of class (*b*) is unfortunate so far as concerns the above statement of comparative values. As an individual work, it comes much closer to the El Greco in formal significance than our discussion would imply; perhaps indeed equals it. We are here concerned, however, not with the evaluation of individual works, but rather with the indication of a general principle.

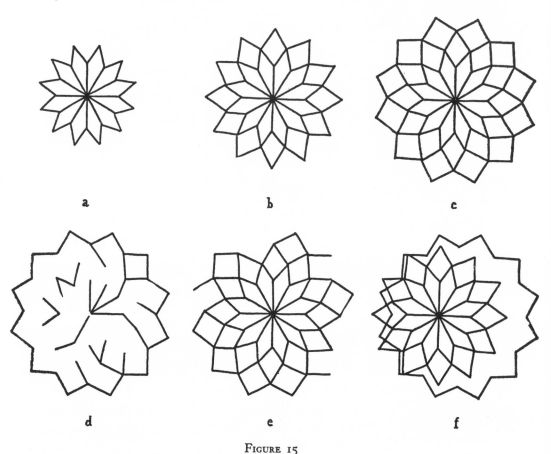

a   b   c

d   e   f

FIGURE 15

DIAGRAMS SYMBOLIZING VARIATIONS OF REPRESENTATIONAL FORM

for their own intrinsic possibilities of organization. Plastically the form of the resulting work is defective; associatively it attains significance. Graphically symbolized, this means that the outer layer of our diagram will remain as before, but that the inner ones will disintegrate, with the result as in (d).

Next we had the opposite case, typified by works like the Manet "Mlle. Victorine," in which the plastic elements are organized but the

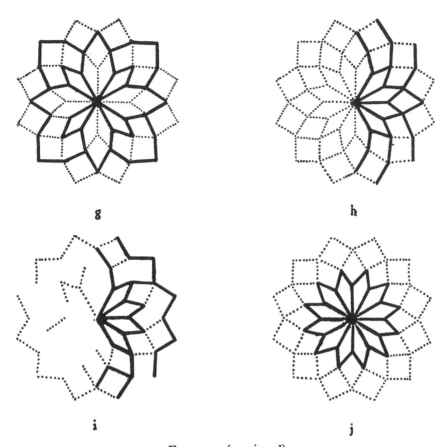

g

h

i

j

FIGURE 15 (*continued*)

DIAGRAMS SYMBOLIZING VARIATIONS OF REPRESENTATIONAL FORM

associative ones are not—or are only partially so. Such works are significant in plastic form but shallow or discordant in associative form. The two inner layers of our diagram will accordingly remain intact, but now the outer one will show breaks or incongruities (*e*).

Finally we noticed the type of work represented by the Degas "Repasseuses," in which both the plastic and the associative components of the form are satisfactory in their respective organizations, but are not satisfactorily interrelated with each other. All the layers of our design will retain their organization, but the outer one will no longer be concentric with the two inner ones. It will start from a different center, so that at some point the two spheres must inevitably overlap and conflict with each other (*f*).

Thus far we have considered only the most general classes of visual organization. Among the infinitely varied reality of art forms, there are, of course, almost infinite variations within each of these classes. One work will have a little more of plastic significance in relation, let us say, to a given amount of associative disorganization; another a little less of plastic significance in relation to a given amount of associative organization.

Apart from differences in degree of organization, further variations will arise through differences in degree of emphasis upon one element or another, or one set of elements and another. Within the general class combining plastic with associative significance, symbolized by diagram (*c*), constant variations will appear as color dominates line or is subordinate to it, as space plays a major or a minor part in the organization, as character sets the motif for action or action the motif for character. For each medium there will be a certain range of more or less ideal patterns. Color will certainly play a more dominant part in painting, for instance, than it does in sculpture or etching; mass will play a more dominant part in sculpture than it does in pictorial art; action will be likely to play a larger part in pictorial art than it does in sculpture.

One of these ideal forms, in which the elements are interrelated with degrees of emphasis corresponding to the natural propensities of the medium, might be symbolized by diagram (*g*). Certain lines in each sphere are made to stand out more strongly than others, but are so interrelated with the others that the balance and harmony of the design remain, while its variety is increased. It is probably this diagram, a refinement upon (*c*), rather than (*c*) itself, which corresponds most closely to our El Greco and also to our Titian and our first Rembrandt. For these works, in their different ways, exhibit more or less ideal scales of emphasis such as we have been discussing.

Conversely there may be placements of emphasis which are displacements from the ideal tension of the given medium. Associative effects may overbalance plastic ones. Certain plastic or associative elements may be "accentuated"; that is to say, may be given more than their ideal part to play in the economy of the form. In this case, we shall again have a stressing of certain elements, but they will be, as it were, the wrong ones instead of the right ones. They will throw the design out of balance or in other ways disturb some of its important relations, as suggested by diagram (*h*). Examples of form showing such displacements from ideal equilibrium might be found, let us say, in certain late Monets, with their accentuation of atmospheric color at the expense of solidity and volume, and in Millet's "Angelus," with its accentuation of associative elements.

The "flamboyance" and "melodrama" which Doctor Barnes charges against Delacroix are usually due, I believe, to a combination of the two disturbing factors which we have now observed: breaks in the organization of either the plastic or the associative components of the form, and displacements of emphasis upon elements good in their place but not properly dominant. As an example, let us consider the "Death of Assurbanipal" in the Louvre (Fig. 16). It contains good plastic passages: the richness of color in the two lower corners, the rhythm and volume of mass in the standing woman in the foreground. But those passages are not parts of a unified context; they are isolated fragments. As a study, complete in itself, the figure mentioned would doubtless be a striking plastic achievement. Taken as a whole, the "Death of Assurbanipal" is not far from plastic confusion.

There are forceful associative passages also, as we see when we study the individual figures or groups. The action of the man struggling with the horse is nobly conceived, the contrast of sex impressive in the two figures in the right foreground. But again the fine passages are fragmentary; they are not parts of a fine context.

And apart from these breaks in the form, is the further defect resulting from the accentuation of associative effects in general and of action in particular. The dramatic action is, in fact, dominant to such a degree that the attention is forcibly, almost violently, recalled to it after every momentary focus upon some other possible source of appeal. Disruption of form and displacement of formal equilibrium in the interest of the dramatic—that is probably close to a definition of the melodramatic. Were I to attempt a symbolical representation of the form of this work, with its double defect of disruption and displacement, the result would be after the fashion of diagram (i).

I suspect that we have here as good a basis as can be found for a differentiation between classic and romantic art in some fundamental sense; which, needless to say, is not, or is only partially, the sense employed when the terms are used as labels for the well-known French schools of the early nineteenth century. Classic art—though the term itself is an unfortunate one, having so many connotations—classic art is that in which the expressive elements are subservient to the formal relations. Romantic art is that in which the formal relations are sub-servient to the expressive elements. The distinction between the two is symbolized by the contrast between the formal perfection of diagram (*g*) and the lapses in form which result from preoccupation with mean-ing in diagrams (*d*) and (*i*).

The sense in which these terms are here used is close to that given to them by Mr. R. H. Wilenski,[2] and I am indebted to him for establish-ing it. But in the terms of our general theory there is hardly so distinct a separation between the two types as I understand him to imply. Form is not necessarily separated from "emotive fragments"—from expressive meanings—and in both classic and romantic art there is usually some combination of the two. But in the former, the form is central and the meanings are valued only as far as they contribute to it; in the latter, the meanings are central and the form is valued only in so far as it con-tributes to them. Hence Delacroix, a romanticist in the deeper as well as in the more limited sense, pursues his dramatic elements without great concern for the resulting effect on the total form, whereas such artists as Giotto and El Greco see in dramatic elements additional notes which can be woven into the form.

Æsthetically, I am inclined to believe that these are the only two fundamental types of art which exist. Truly descriptive or photo-graphic art would have no artistic form at all, being merely a reproduc-tion of existing objects, and scientific rather than æsthetic in its intent —if it had any intent beyond the pleasure of its creator in the act of reproduction. If it developed any æsthetic values, they would be essen-tially either formal or expressive. Depending upon which took the nuclear position, it would assume a classic or a romantic tinge. Mr.

---

[2] *Cf. The Modern Movement in Art*, Part I.

Wilenski's category of "religious" art also appears to me non-æsthetic and capable of resolution into productions either classic or romantic in æsthetic principle. Similarly with such terms as "naturalism" and "realism." As I understand them, they deal with the non-æsthetic consideration of the degree to which the meanings involved in a work are literal, not with the æsthetic one of the relation which those meanings bear to the embracing form.

Two further categories of artistic effect which are frequently differentiated from each other in critical literature are the "decorative" and the "expressive." The distinction between them is concisely stated by Doctor Barnes and Miss de Mazia in *The Art of Henri-Matisse.* "Design is of two sorts, 'expressive' and 'decorative.' Expressive design aims to reveal the artist's individual grasp of what is essential in his subject-matter. Decorative design aims at immediate charm in the work of art and is not intended to convey any interpretation of the deeper aspects of things. . . . It is by expressive design that a sense of the deep human values of experience is conveyed. In decoration the value resides in satisfaction of our need to perceive abundantly and freely."[3] The authors add that a combination of these two types of design, organically fused, is essential to the greatest works of art. Mr. Cheney draws much the same distinction, characterizing decorative form by its dominantly "sensuous" appeal, and expressive form by its more profound "emotional content," its heightened and more elusive æsthetic significance, which he calls its "fourth-dimensional" quality.[4]

In the terms of our present analysis, "decorative" and "expressive" design reduce themselves simply to two levels of amplitude in representational form. The æsthetic distinction between them is quantitative

[3] P. 17.   [4] *Cf. A Primer of Modern Art,* pp. 52–55.

rather than qualitative; a distinction in comparative richness of effect rather than in kind or in aim. Fundamentally both pursue the same aim: to use representational elements for the creation of visual form. But one employs a greater range of elements, creates a correspondingly more complex and subtle form, and consequently affords a more significant and moving experience.

In its original and literal sense, the term "decorative" refers, of course, to designs used for purposes of decoration; designs which, instead of being complete and self-determined works of art, are details in a more inclusive whole, as mural paintings or portal carvings are details in the total effect of a building. In such cases, the picture or statue gives up its independent existence to merge into the larger whole. Its form is not a self-determined entity, but is one of the elements to be combined in creating a more inclusive form. As in all form construction, the element must follow the law of the whole; the mural must subserve the governing architectural effect, the vase painting must subserve the vase. Usually this means that the work decoratively employed must sacrifice a portion of its own potential effect in order to take its proper place in the context of relations of which it has become a part. Sufficient flatness to preserve the effect of the underlying structural surfaces, sufficient formality to harmonize with the surrounding structural lines and shapes, and sufficient boldness to achieve the necessary "carrying power," are the most common of the requirements which it is called upon to fulfil.

In the course of time, the resulting pattern-like form, with its emphasis upon clear-cut design and simple striking color effects, has won a place for itself in the affections of the art-loving world. It has been cultivated by certain artists from choice rather than necessity. The term "decorative" has thus come to have a larger and more general meaning, applying to any work of a more or less stylized, and in painting more or less two-dimensional, character; any work, in other words, which possesses or recalls the qualities originally imposed upon representational art by decorative necessities. Gauguin's work provides the standard modern example.

"Decorative" effects, then, are those produced by representational form when purposely arrested at a certain level of amplitude, either by external requirements which impose a pattern-like effect or from a spontaneous interest in producing such an effect. Partly because of their "priority" in visual media, partly as a result of the structural necessities already noticed, the elements emphasized are the second-stratum plastic ones, color, line, and shape. The elements most strongly subordinated are the third-stratum plastic ones, particularly mass and space because of their emphasis upon the third dimension. The more elusive ranges of fourth-dimensional meanings are also largely eliminated, since they are inconsistent with the desired effect of simplicity, formality, and more or less obvious surface charm. This decorative type of form is symbolized in diagram (j). The three layers corresponding to the second, third, and fourth strata are all present, organized, and integrated, but the two outer layers are both subordinated to the inner or second-stratum one.

This conception of decorative form explains all the characteristics commonly associated with decorative work. The latter gives little insight into "the deeper aspects of things" because associative elements are subordinate in it, and because the limited amplitude of the form does not provide strong reinforcement for those expressive elements which may actually be present. It produces an effect of "charm" rather than of "power" because of that same limited amplitude, arresting formal experience at the point of pleasantness instead of carrying it on to that of rapture or profound stirring. It is dominantly "sensuous" because the second-stratum element, color, plays so large a part in it and is used so largely for the simpler bolder effects which emphasize its quality as material.

"Expressive" design can be dealt with more shortly. We have, in fact, already studied it at length, for it is simply representational form free of all external limitations and cultivated for its own maximum richness. It is found in work of that inclusive, fully organized type which we have symbolized by diagram (c) and more exactly still by diagram (g). It conveys "deep human values" because it employs to their maximum all the resources of fourth-stratum expressiveness and reinforces that expressiveness with maximum formal power. To call it "fourth-dimensional" is to employ a bold figure, but one expressive of the elusive complexity of its relations and the compelling and mysterious power by which it moves us. The greatest work involves both "decorative" and "expressive" aspects, integrated with each other, because the latter are necessarily an expansion from the former; because maximum form can exist only when all the artistic strata make their individual contributions and when those contributions are co-ordinated in the total context of relations.

In view of these considerations, it seems safe to say that we must avoid any tendency to think of "decorative" and "expressive" effects as different from each other in kind or in ultimate aim, and must recognize them as different amplifications of a common representational form. "Perhaps," writes Mr. Cheney, "the sensuous impression afforded by an absolute decoration is a sort of first dimension of the

deeper ecstasy that is afforded by a picture indubitably rich in volumi-
nous form." This seems to me certainly to be the case. The "decorative" merges into the "expressive" by imperceptible degrees as representational form expands in the range of its elements, in consequent
amplitude, and in resultant power to stir the sense of beauty.

That being the case, it may be doubted whether the "satisfaction of
our need to perceive abundantly and freely" should be thought of as
distinguishing between the decorative and the expressive types of form.
All form, decorative and expressive alike, takes its value from its power
to satisfy perceptive needs. Indeed, form might be defined, in its psychological aspect, as that organization of materials which fits them for
perception.

The distinction between the two types of form under consideration
lies in the *degree of fullness* to which perceptive needs are satisfied.
In decorative form, the relations being fewer and more obvious, we
grasp them more easily and as a result enjoy them in lighter fashion.
We might well apply to decorative effect Professor Dewey's remark
concerning the "fanciful": "The material is too slight to call forth the
full energy of the dispositions in which values and meanings are embodied; it does not offer enough resistance, and so the mind plays with
it capriciously." [5] Possibly the word "capriciously" is too strong for
the present context. Otherwise no better characterization of decorative
form could be found.

In expressive form, the relations are subtler and more numerous;
they draw more heavily upon our perceptive powers and consequently
afford us, when mastered, a more deeply moving experience. The "resistance" is greater and the mind, challenged to go beyond the limits of

[5] *Art as Experience,* p. 268.

"capricious play," throws into its perceptive activity "the full energy of the dispositions in which values and meanings are embodied."

Corresponding differences of amplitude occur in all the arts and indeed in every phase of experience. Such, to one degree or another, are the differences between Tchaikovsky's "Nutcracker Suite" and Beethoven's Ninth Symphony, between Shelley's "To a Skylark" and "Hamlet," between the Ca' d'Oro and the cathedral of Chartres. Such also are differences between a game easily taken and one which calls forth the player's maximum skill and endurance; between the light allurements of a flirtation and the soul-engrossing passion of profound love. In all such cases, the lower or introductory levels of experience are accompanied by milder pleasures; the higher or culminating levels, by the more intense emotions of triumph and ecstasy. And the more intense the emotion, the greater the heightening of reality felt by the one experiencing it.

The greater "reality" of expressive as compared with decorative art, I should ascribe to a similar cause: the relevancy of the work to a more profoundly moving experience. Indeed, we can follow the rise from one level of effect to the other in our contemplation of many great works of architecture. Decorative features such as mosaics and stained-glass windows, even though limited to a decorative significance when observed in isolation, become impregnated with expressive power when seen as details in an all-embracing total effect. Conversely we sometimes experience the loss of expressive possibilities and the descent to a purely decorative level when such details are removed from their original architectural stations and exhibited individually in museums.

To reach an entirely accurate statement of the relation of these two types of form to perceptive experience, I believe that we should split the phrase quoted above. Decorative form assists us to perceive "freely," in the sense of easily and pleasantly, but it is expressive form which enables us to perceive most "abundantly," if by that term we mean deeply and intensely.

It might seem, in considering the "Death of Assurbanipal" (Fig. 16), that we could here detect what we failed to find in our earlier study of associative effects—a type of subject-matter (that is a type of expressive meaning) which is genuinely unfit for visual representation because inevitably destructive to the harmony of visual form. I refer to any type of subject-matter which is extremely powerful in its emotional expressiveness; so powerful, it might seem, that it cannot be subjected to the discipline of form. Subjects which give unbridled expression to primary instincts, as the "Assurbanipal" gives expression to the terror of death struggles and pornographic art sometimes gives expression to sex, would be the chief ones involved. We might suppose that such subjects, like the wildest beasts and the proudest men, resist captivity to the point of extinction, breaking either themselves or their aggressors before they will cease their struggle for independence. To call such subjects "literary" would be an affront to literature, for that art also has its melodrama and allows it no higher standing than do its visual sisters. We could only describe them as intractable to use in art.

In their extremes of unbridled expressiveness I am inclined to believe that such subjects are beyond the power of art to control, but if their expressiveness has been given extreme development, that is as much as to say that we are in the presence of a romantic conception and probably an undeveloped and therefore relatively weak form. As pure types of subject-matter, as representations of this or that type of event, I doubt whether even they can be categorically excluded from significant art. Episodes from Michelangelo's "Last Judgment," Tintoretto's "Crucifixions" and some of his battle scenes, Rubens' scenes of hunting and battle, certain works by Goya, and Rembrandt's occasional etchings of sexual subjects, certainly give pause to a hasty exclusion of powerful types of subject-matter simply because they are powerful. The expressive elements in such works are strong, but the form is stronger, dominating them for its own enrichment.

We are faced here with the measure of the artist's form-building powers. If Gericault's "Raft of the Medusa" is melodramatic, Michelangelo's representation of the bark of Charon is not so, though it employs subject-matter similar in many of its elements. Any subject which an artist can subjugate to form is, æsthetically, a proper subject for art and the great pictorial dramatists have already subjugated materials so powerful that one may well be wary of assuming any absolute limits to their powers in this respect. At any rate those limits are at higher voltage than the subject of the "Death of Assurbanipal." I am confident that Rubens could have formally mastered this subject if he had cared to essay it; indeed, that Delacroix himself could have done so, had he developed under influences which strengthened, rather than weakened, his concentration on form.

Apart from the genius of the artist, the capacities of the medium also do much to determine what subject-matter can be effectively mastered. A medium can absorb only those types of subject with which its physical qualities have expressive affinities. There must be ranges of expression common to the two, before they can adequately unite. Painting, with its greater range of plastic elements and its infinite capacity for the subordination of detail, dominates many subjects which would appear theatrical in sculpture. Graphic arts, with their wiry lightness, succeed with subjects, particularly those involving humor and caricature, which painting usually renders heavy and which in turn often render it ostentatious. Sculpture, perhaps because of its independence of color and its concentration on compact forms, shares something of this graphic waywardness and has consorted with the grotesque more successfully than painting.

Whatever the theoretical limits of art in these respects, they are in any case unimportant compared to its actual summits of attainment, which lie nearer the center of its field. We may return to, and at the same time take leave of, our main theme by reasserting the balance of plastic and associative values in a governing formal significance which is characteristic of the greatest representational art. When one turns from the "Death of Assurbanipal" to Giotto's "Nativity" or Titian's "St. Jerome," to Veronese's "Rape of Europa" or El Greco's "Agony," that balance seems perhaps their most striking characteristic. Whatever the nature of the subject, one feels immediately a sense of repose and serenity. One is struck by an atmosphere of "classic restraint"; reassured by a feeling that "God's in his heaven; all's right with the world." An immediate impression of order expands, as one contemplates the work, into a perception of form omnipresent and omnipotent.

And upon whatever passage of the work the eye may rest, it finds that passage fused of plastic and associative significance. If it delights in a line, it cannot long remain oblivious to the significance of the gesture which that line, perhaps, helps to define. If it is arrested by the significance of that gesture, it cannot long restrain the necessity of

Fig. 16. Delacroix. Death of Assurbanipal
Louvre. (Giraudon)

admiring the line by which it is defined. And the mind and spirit, to which the eye is a servant, know in their delight neither plastic nor associative boundaries. They recognize the work before them as an undivided visual world, heightened in the grace of every aspect of visual reality.

CHAPTER X

CONCLUSIONS

We have reached the end of our study of form and representation. What are our conclusions? They may be summarized under four headings.

1. Æsthetic values, as Santayana and earlier critics maintained, are of three categories, those of material, form, and expression. Form is thus not the exclusive source of such values. As our analysis has indicated, however, it is the dominant source, for ultimately it absorbs the other two. Material and expression alike, though potentially beautiful in themselves, become elements of the form in which they are employed. The appropriateness of any given sensuous or expressive quality is relative to the context of relations into which it is woven. Though it may possess intrinsic beauty, that particular type of beauty becomes undesirable, a source in fact of ugliness, if its relations with other elements of the embracing form are discordant. Thus form becomes the determining factor in the beauty of a work of art.

Representation, on the other hand, is not intrinsically æsthetic; subject-matter, merely as such, is void of æsthetic value. It can affect such value, if at all, only in the relation of means to end; only through some enrichment which it brings to beauties of material, of form, or of expression.

Thus far our conclusions are in substantial agreement with the views of Mr. Bell and the abstractionists. Form is the dominant source of æsthetic value; representation is non-æsthetic. What the creative modern painters rediscovered for art, the abstractionist critics helped to formulate for criticism, and their insistence on the prime significance of form has rendered valuable service to the cause of beauty and to the comprehension of art.

But if our further conclusions are tenable, they only partially grasped their own principles. In asserting that subject-matter was "irrelevant" to æsthetic effect, in assuming that the ideal of visual art lay in geometrical abstraction, they reacted against one extreme by going to another almost equally far from the truth. They represented in criticism what Cubism did in art: the pursuit of a theory to what seemed its logical conclusion but proved to be a demonstration of the inexactitude of its premises. Maintained at its extreme, their theory resulted in loss rather than gain. The real prophets of form in modern art, the creators who gave visual form the richest and loftiest embodiments it has yet found in the modern world, were not Picasso and Braque in their Cubistic experiments, but earlier artists such as Manet, Renoir, and Cézanne; artists whose work was definitely representational. Judged in relation to the work of these men, Cubism was not a progress but a retrogression.

As with the artist, so with the critic; the whole truth had not been apprehended on the level of abstractionism. For abstractionist criticism assumed two things which our study would seem to have demonstrated false: first, that plastic and representational elements were sharply separable from each other and formed two mutually exclusive spheres of effect; secondly, that the plastic elements in some unexplained way had a monopoly over formal beauty and that the only significant form was plastic form. With these assumptions, our remaining conclusions oblige us to differ.

2. The plastic elements do not constitute a sphere of vision which is apprehensible to the mind through pure visual sensation or which, in its full range, can be embodied in art without recourse to representation. Only colors, lines, flat shapes, and sizes, are directly perceptible without interpretation through non-visual experience, and only they are possible in painting without representation. Sculpture, by virtue of its solid materials, can add the third dimension without necessarily becoming representational. Purely abstract art would thus be limited to geometrical pattern in painting, and to a three-dimensional grouping of geometrical masses in sculpture. Apart from the plastic limitations thus imposed, the continued production of significant abstract forms proves to be difficult. The elements are so few and conventional that the mind soon exhausts its power of achieving fresh results with them.

Representation overcomes both these limitations. It contributes new plastic elements such as space and illumination. It opens the way for an influx of natural motifs which continually reinspire creative invention, leading to forms which would not otherwise be conceived and which are potentially richer than those that would otherwise be conceived. Thus representation is not in conflict with the development of plastic form, but is essential to that development. Plastic values are potentially greater in representational art than in abstract art. The masterpieces of plastic form are not, in fact, abstract; they are representational.

3. Form is not essentially tangible or physical or plastic in its nature. It is not a kind of body opposed to a content or spirit. It is rather a life informing a body, an organizing principle which brings elements into significant relationship with each other. Its beauty results from the quality of the relationship rather than from the nature of the elements related.

Representation is not in any sense the antithesis of form, which would be formlessness or lack of relationship, nor is it unamenable to form. Representation is merely a source of elements and these elements, even when ultra-plastic or "associative," present themselves to form as potential materials to be related. There can, in short, be associative as well as plastic form. Even more, there can be interrelations between plastic *and* associative elements. The total form of the greatest works of painting and sculpture is a plastic-associative, or representational, form. Such form alone is capable of pressing formal beauty to the maximum range and richness attainable in visual art.

This conclusion supports what we earlier called the "middle position" with regard to our problem and for the first time, if I am not mistaken, makes possible an entirely logical statement of that position. As indicated in our opening section, earlier statements suffered from one or the other of two limitations. Some frankly recognized a seeming paradox in their demand for both form and representation, putting their faith in the "common sense" of æsthetic experience and maintaining their position in spite of the abstractionist views which, critically, they could not refute. Others proposed solutions which, in view of internal inconsistencies or limitation to certain types of art, proved to be only partial and inadequate.

As a result of the present study, we are now, I believe, in possession of logical grounds upon which to support the middle position. We are able to formulate the æsthetic principles upon which it rests and to demonstrate the validity of those principles by critical analysis of all the aspects and variations of representational art.

And it may be observed that the solution which we thus propose to the problem of form and subject-matter, is in some sense a common denominator of the conflicting views summarized in our introduction. As already noted it is in agreement with Mr. Bell's assertion that form is the ultimate source of æsthetic significance in art. At the same time, it upholds the fundamental tenet of the middle position, as stated by writers like Doctor Barnes and Doctor Reid, that the highest æsthetic significance demands a fusion of form and subject-matter. Finally our position incorporates the third important hypothesis which has been advanced concerning the matter: that of psychological (or what we have called "associative") form developed by Messrs. Mauron and Fry. In the light of our analysis, these three views merge as aspects of a single larger truth.

4. To our first three conclusions, we may add a fourth and more general one: that visual experience, in its psychological roots as well as in its ultimate artistic developments, is essentially representational and, in this respect, essentially different from aural experience. As our chief guide to spatial and tangible reality, vision is inseparably linked for us with things. Hence visual stimuli are highly charged with object-suggesting associations. We are obliged forcibly to resist these associa-

tions if we wish to prevent them from crystallizing into the definition of objects.

Of hearing, the reverse is true. Sounds appear to us by their nature disembodied, detached from tangible existence. Very few sounds have any object-suggesting associations. Even those which do, like bird songs, are not thought of as being part of the suggested objects but merely as fleeting vibrations produced by them. For the most part sound can become representational only through the purely arbitrary process of language formation, in which meanings are attached to sounds having no intrinsic relation to them and no direct connection with external reality.

This basic difference in the elements provided to the mind by sight and hearing continues and expands when combinations of such elements are used for the creation of artistic form. Visual form is fundamentally representational (or in architecture and the industrial arts, functional, an analogous qualification); musical form is fundamentally abstract. Hence the representational works of a Fourth Dynasty Egyptian sculptor, a Phidias, or a Maillol, of a Giotto, a Titian, or a Cézanne, stand as the summits of art in sculpture and painting, while the abstract symphonic forms of a Bach, a Beethoven, or a Brahms mark the summits of art in music. We should work an irreparable loss were we to eliminate representation in the first case or to impose it in the second.

This being the case, we must recognize a confusion of thought in the idea that the representational arts should strive to imitate the abstractness or "purity" of musical form. We cannot accept the abstractionist statement, referred to by Mr. Cheney and quoted in our introductory section, that "There is no more reason . . . why painting should be dependent upon the . . . suggestion of natural objects than there is for music to be dependent upon likeness to natural sounds." As we have observed, there is a very fundamental reason why the two arts mentioned should pursue opposite principles in this respect.

All form is "pure," whether it be abstract or representational. Form is relationship, organization; and organization is always pure. But what determines the æsthetic significance of form is its relative amplitude—its range, richness, variety, complexity. The true ideal set by music for the other arts lies not in its abstractness, an incidental consideration, but in its marvellous richness. That richness, because of the nature of its medium, it can most successfully cultivate in the realm of abstraction. To attain a similar richness, painting and sculpture must definitely avoid abstraction. Only when they employ their innate resources of spontaneously evoked meanings do they present a sufficient variety of elements, a sufficient range and complexity of relations, to make possible the achievement of forms worthy to compare with symphonic music in exalted beauty.

INDEX

INDEX

Abstract form, two dimensional, 35 ff.; three dimensional, 45 ff., 163; limitations of, 48 ff., 117–18, 163–4.

Abstractionist criticism, 2 ff., 9 ff., 60–61, 163–4, 167.

"Accentuation," 149.

Action, 81 ff.

Æsthetic values, three classes of, 19, 21, 162; relation between three classes, 69 ff.; relative significance of three classes, 32–3, 68 ff.

"Amplitudes" of form, see Form.

Architecture, 46–7.

Arts, relations between the, 99–100.

Association, 19–21, 62–4, 67; "objectification" of, 20–21, 66–7.

Associative effects, their place in visual art, 93 ff., 118–20.

Associative form, definition of, 72–3; origins of the conception, 121; relation to plastic form, 93 ff., 122 ff.

Attention, focus of, 93 ff.; alternating process of, 96–7.

Barnes, Albert C., 6 ff., 105, 132–3, 152, 166.

Bell, Clive, 2, 3, 5.

Bergson, Henri, 6.

Cézanne, 10, 12, 60.

Character, a form, 75 ff., 123; relations between characters, 79 ff.

Cheney, Sheldon, 2, 13, 152, 155.

Classicism, definition of, 150–51.

Color, 26 ff.; the individual color, 26 ff.; color relations, 30; relation to form, 33–4.

Content, 15, 91–2.

Continuum of experience, 95.

Crivelli, "Annunciation," 90.

Croce, Benedetto, 15, 92.

Cubism, 3, 47–8, 52–3, 118.

Decoration, 12, 104, 152 ff.

Degas, "Repasseuses," 144.

Delacroix, 8; "Death of Assurbanipal," 149 ff., 158.

De Mazia, Violette, 152.

Dewey, John, 49, 156.

"Displacement" of formal equilibrium, 149–50.

Dramatic effect, 88–9, 150.

El Greco, 13; "Agony in the Garden," 85 ff., 111, 128 ff.

Expression, definition of, 19–21; æsthetic and non-æsthetic, 20–21, 66–7; in color, 28, 125–30; in form, 31–2; non-visual sources of, 44, 65; enrichment of form through, 45.

"Expressive design," 152, 155 ff.

Form (see also Associative, Functional, Plastic, and Representational form), definition of, 19, 21–3, 165; various "amplitudes" of, 31–2, 45, 58–60, 71–3, 75 ff., 97–8, 124 ff., 144 ff., 168; relation to subject-matter, 1, 91–2; compared with other sources of æsthetic value, 32, 68–9; enrichment through expression, 45; through ultra-plastic representation, 69 ff.; "displacement" of, 149–50.

Fry, Roger, 15, 121–2.

Functional form, 46–7, 51.

"Fusion" between subject-matter and "body-forms," 14–15.

Geometrical pattern, 35–8.

Giorgione, 13; "Pastoral Concert," 5.

Giotto, 13, 131–2.

Guillaume and Monro, 7.

Holmes, Sir Charles, 6–7.

Illumination, 42.

Illustration, 11, 108.

Impressionism, 94.

Industrial form, 46–7, 51.

"Internal" as distinguished from "ultra-pictorial" meanings, 106 ff.

Knowledge as related to æsthetic experience, 105, 111–12.

Light, 42.

"Literary" effects in visual art, 98 ff., 141 ff.

Literary form, 99 ff., 136 ff.

Manet, 104.

Material, beauty of, defined, 19; relation to form, 33–4; enriched through form, 32–3; through expression, 64–5.

Mathematical form, 33.

Mather, Frank Jewett, 5–6.
Matisse, 12–13.
Mauron, Charles, 15, 76, 121.
Meanings, "internal" as distinguished from "ultra-pictorial," 106 ff.; universal as distinguished from particular, 114–16.
Melodrama, 8, 149–50, 159; definition of, 150.
"Middle position" in modern criticism, 54–5, 165–6.
Millais, "Lorenzo and Isabella," 107, 141.
Music, 2–3, 39–40, 122, 137.

Naturalism, 152.
Nature as source of creative inspiration, 58–9.
"Network of relations," 22, 60, 79.
Non-visual experience as related to vision, 41 ff., 97–8.

Paleolithic art, 7.
Pattern, two types of, 35; geometrical, 35–8; limitations of, 35 ff.; representational, 58–9.
Perception, 31–2.
Perugino, "Agony in the Garden," 86, 130–31.
"Photographic" art, 151.
Plastic effects, partly representational, 58–61, 164; not the sole source of visual form, 90–91; relation to associative effects, 135 ff.
Plastic "equivalency," 9 ff., 13, 124.
Plastic form, enriched through representation, 60–61, 164–5; relation to associative form, 122 ff.
Poetry, 123.
"Priority," of elements in visual form, 136–8.
"Psychological form," 15, 73, 76.

Raphael, "Marriage of the Virgin," 78.
Realism, 152.
"Reality" in æsthetic experience, 157–8.
Reid, Herbert Arnaud, 4, 14, 166.
Relations, "network of," 22, 60, 79.
Rembrandt, "Portrait of an Old Woman," 75, 82, 115–6; "Portrait of the Painter's Mother," 77, 83.
Representation (see also Ultra-plastic representation), definition of, 56; spontaneous emergence of, 52, 56–7; importance as compared with plastic effects, 135 ff.; relation to plastic effects, 60–61, 93 ff., 135 ff., 164–5; relation to æsthetic values, 24, 58 ff., 118–19; relation to form, 91–2, 165; relation to observer's knowledge, 112–13; internal clarity of, 105 ff., 111–12; confusion due to un-certain, 37, 50; universal and particular meanings in, 114–16; ultra-pictorial extensions of, 105 ff., 116 ff.
Representational form, definition of, 73, 124–5, 134; examples of, 125 ff.; variations of, 135 ff.; defective examples of, 142 ff.
Romanticism, definition of, 150–51.

Santayana, George, 19–21, 69, 121.
Sculpture, 59, 160.
Sensation, visual, 26–7; tactile, 64–5.
Sensuous appeal of color, 27; of texture, 43; through ultra-plastic representation, 64–5.
Setting, 81 ff.
"Significant form," 2, 3.
Social background of art, 116–17.
Sound, intrinsically abstract, 39–40, 167–8.
Space, 52.
"Strata" of vision, 25; first stratum, 26 ff.; second stratum, 29 ff., 57–8; third stratum, 41 ff., 57; fourth stratum, 62 ff., 90 ff.
Subject-matter, see Representation.

Tactile sensation, 43, 64–5.
Texture, 43–4.
Third dimension, 42.
Tintoretto, 8, 13, 103; "Annunciation," 84.
Titian, 13, 132; "Entombment," 5; compared with Cézanne, "Still Life," 10, 132–3; "Madonna of the Cherries," 79, 83–4, 106, 127; "Presentation of the Virgin," 80.
"Transferred values," 13.

Ultra-pictorial representation, 105 ff.
Ultra-plastic representation, effect on "material," 64–5; effect on form, 69 ff.; effect on expression, 65 ff.; place in visual art, 97 ff., 118–20.
Universal as distinguished from particular meanings, 114–16.

Velasquez, 104.
Vermeer, 104.
Veronese, "Marriage of St. Catherine," 84.
Vision, intrinsically representational, 39–40, 167; affected by non-visual experience, 41 ff., 90 ff., 97–8; priority of elements in, 136 ff.
Visual form, various "amplitudes" of, see Form.

Wilenski, R. H., 151–2.